In Defiance of The Elements

In Defiance of The Elements
John Moorehead
photographs by Robin Constable

Namara Publications

HIS HIGHNESS SHEIKH KHALIFA BIN HAMAD AL THANI EMIR OF THE STATE OF QATAR

This edition published by
Namara Publications Limited 1980
Namara House
45-46 Poland Street, London w1

First published by
Quartet Books Limited 1977
a member of the Namara Group
27 Goodge Street, London w1

Design by Mike Jarvis, Jim Wire

ISBN 0 7043 2149 1

Printed in Great Britain by
Gavin Martin Limited, London SE 27
and bound by Mansell Limited, Witham, Essex

An aerial view of Doha, the capital of Qatar.

HIS HIGHNESS SHEIKH HAMAD BIN KHALIFA AL THANI,
HEIR APPARENT, MINISTER OF DEFENCE & COMMANDER-IN-CHIEF OF THE ARMED FORCES

Contents

Part One
Qatar in History

The First Settlers

On 11 October 1939 the British Political agent in Bahrain sent the following telegram to his opposite number in Kuwait:
'PETROLEUM DEVELOPMENT QATAR HAVE HAD SLIGHT SHOW OF OIL IN THEIR TEST WELL NEAR ZEKRIT STOP DRILLING CONTINUES.'

It is not often that one can pin down the precise moment when the fortunes of a country are suddenly and dramatically changed, but for Qatar, a bleak and rugged strip of desert in the Arabian Gulf, this was undoubtedly it. The news of an oil strike came at a particularly desperate time in Qatar's history. For centuries the local people had been almost totally dependent on the rich pearl banks of the Gulf for their livelihood. A few Bedouin tribesmen wandered through the peninsula and others made their living as fishermen. But it was the pearl trade which had always supported the small communities dotted round the coast of Qatar. In the early 1930s a catastrophe suddenly overtook these people. An economic recession in the West and the introduction of the Japanese cultured pearl combined to ruin the trade almost overnight. All along the coast of the Gulf men found themselves out of work. Qatar, with no other resources, was severely hit, and large numbers of people took to their boats and sailed to other countries.

The discovery of oil in 1939 did not immediately change the situation. The war intervened and it was some time before the country began to reap the benefits of this unexpected windfall. But less than twenty-five years after the British agent's succinct telegram announcing the oil strike, Qatar had emerged from abject poverty to boundless prosperity.

It was an experience unparalleled in the history of a country where the people had always had to struggle merely to survive. The barren landscape of the peninsula, its climate and geographical position – all these things singled it out as perhaps one of the least habitable places on earth.

Qatar is situated almost exactly half-way up the western coast of the Arabian Gulf. It is instantly identifiable on a map because it juts out from the coast for eighty miles to form a thumb-shaped peninsula about the same size, for instance, as Jamaica. To the north, east and west it is surrounded by the sea; to the south it shares a border with Saudi Arabia and Abu Dhabi, and here, at the neck of the peninsula, there is a series of depressions which suggests that Qatar may once long ago have been an island. This was the conclusion that the two explorers, St John Philby and Bertram Thomas, came to when they travelled through the area in the 1930s. It is only twenty miles from coast to coast at the base of the peninsula, and in the past it was said that three men stationed at strategic intervals could watch the whole southern border from sea to sea.

The interior of Qatar consists of a flat stony desert stretching from one end of the country to the other. Hardly a single feature of note relieves the monotony of the landscape. Along the coast, however, the sea runs through a whole spectrum of colours from dark blue to brilliant aquamarine, as it ripples round the endless sand-banks, reefs and shoals which lie off-shore. The peninsula is very hot and dry. It has less than five inches of rain a year and, in the summer, the temperature is constantly over 100°F (38°C). In the winter it is surprisingly cool. The north wind blows in continuously from the sea, and although the sun shines all day long, the air is sharp and clear.

Perhaps it is the dead unchanging character of the desert which makes Qatar seem like a very old country. Certainly it has been inhabited by men from the very earliest times. Recent archaeological discoveries have shown that the first settlers came to the peninsula sometime in the Old Stone Age – at least 50,000 years ago. Much later, about 5,000 years ago, it was inhabited by hunters and fishermen. The rock engravings found in the north of Qatar probably date from this period. Some of the engravings are of animals, others are merely a series of splayed lines which have been variously interpreted as oared boats or scorpions. By about 1000 B.C. the local people were beginning to widen their horizons. The pottery discovered in several tombs dating from this period indicates that they had, by then, been drawn into the life of South-West Asia.

At this point, when our knowledge of other parts of the world begins to fill out, Qatar's past remains inscrutable and little is heard of the peninsula for the next seventeen centuries. Herodotus mentioned it briefly, as did later Arab geographers, and when Islam swept over Arabia, Qatar was one of the first places to accept the new religion. Several early Islamic sites have been identified, showing that in the eighth and ninth centuries the people had extensive contacts with other parts of ·Asia and even China.

In 1497 the Portuguese explorer, Vasco da Gama, rounded the Cape of Good Hope, and European ships appeared in the Gulf for the first time. For centuries the Gulf had been one of the great maritime highways linking East and West; now its southern coastline became strategically important as a series of staging posts was established on the route to India and the East. But although the Portuguese were active in the Gulf, the peninsula was largely ignored by them, and by their successors in the East, the British and the Dutch. Nor did the area count for much in the competition for supremacy among the local powers, Persia, Turkey and Oman.

It was only in the second half of the eighteenth century that Qatar emerged at last from centuries of obscurity. By then, a few meagre settlements had already been established on the east coast at Doha (known at the time as Bida), Wakrah, Fuwairet and Huwailah. The rest of the peninsula was uninhabited except by a few Bedouin tribesmen. To this unpromising land there came in 1766 a completely new people: leaving their homes in Kuwait, a branch of the Utub tribe called the Al Khalifa suddenly migrated *en masse* to Qatar and settled at Zubara on the north-west coast. Here they were followed by the Al Jalahima, another section of the same tribe. The two clans soon fell out with each other and the later arrivals moved further up the coast, first to the village of Ruwais and then to Khor Hassan.

Long before their appearance in Qatar, the Al Khalifa were known throughout the Gulf as skilled sailors and traders, and before long Zubara became a flourishing commercial port. Situated half-way between the entrance and the head of the Gulf, the town was ideally placed to capture the local trade. And on its doorstep were the rich pearl fisheries over which the new settlers soon gained control. Zubara's growing prosperity was further stimulated in 1776 by the Persian siege and eventual capture of Basra from the Turks. Basra was the commercial capital of the northern Gulf and much of its lucrative trade, together with a number of leading merchants, moved to Zubara during the siege.

Thirty miles across the sea in the islands of Bahrain, which were then in the hands of the Persians, these developments were watched with alarm. Zubara presented a direct challenge to the commerce of the islands and from as early as 1777 several unsuccessful expeditions were launched against the Al Khalifa stronghold. The Persian Empire, however, was beginning to

weaken. Taking advantage of the situation, the Al Khalifa attacked Bahrain in 1782, plundered the main town of Manamah and retired to Zubara with a captured ship. This led to war between the Persians and the Al Khalifa in which the latter emerged victorious in 1783.

From then on, the Al Khalifa made Bahrain their capital and the town became one of the most important commercial centres in the Gulf. The Al Khalifa fleet carried much of the trade between Basra and Muscat, sometimes venturing even as far afield as India, from which they brought back silk, cloth, sugar and spices. These goods were paid for with pearls sold in the markets of Muscat. Zubara was inevitably eclipsed by Bahrain at this time, but it still remained a prosperous community, serving as an outlet for trade to Central Arabia. The town consisted of about 400 houses crowded round the shore and protected by a citadel set back inland on slightly higher ground. From this point, a commanding view could be had of the sea to the west and north, and of the desert stretching away to the south and east. Today the site is deserted except for a renovated fort, but it is still possible to imagine the sentries scanning the horizons of the sea and desert for the first sign of a hostile fleet or a marauding horde of Bedouin.

Rahmah bin Jabir

But for the moment it was the Al Jalahima at Khor Hassan, rather than the Al Khalifa in Zubara, who were to hold the centre of the stage in Qatar. The Al Jalahima had taken part in the invasion of Bahrain, but soon quarrelled with their allies once again, claiming they had not received their due share of the spoils of victory. The tribe returned to Khor Hassan, and here a bitter struggle for power took place between Abdulla and Rahmah bin Jabir, two sons of the sheikh who had led the original migration to Qatar. Abdulla, the eldest, eventually got the worst of it and fled to Muscat, leaving his younger brother Rahmah in undisputed control of the tribe.

Thus began the career of a man who was destined to become the most notorious and daring pirate of his time. The early years of the nineteenth century were the hey-day of piracy in the Gulf. By 1809 the coastal Arabs had sixty-three large ships and 19,000 men employed in harrying the local shipping. But among their numbers there was not one to compare with Rahmah bin Jabir for enterprise, courage and ruthlessness. His appearance was equal to his reputation, as the European traveller, Buckingham, discovered when he met him in his declining years. Buckingham wrote:

'Rahmah-ben-Jaber's figure presented a meagre trunk, with four lank members, all of them cut and hacked, and pierced with wounds of sabres, spears and bullets, in every part, to the number perhaps of more than twenty wounds. He had, besides, a face naturally ferocious and ugly, and now rendered still more so by several scars there, and by the loss of one eye.'

Buckingham goes on to give an example of Rahmah's cruelty:

'An instance is related of his having recently put a great number of his own crew, who used mutinous expressions, into a tank on board in which they usually kept their water, and this being shut close at the top, the poor wretches were all suffocated, and afterwards thrown overboard.'

Rahmah's base at Khor Hassan was the ideal pirate's lair. A fort built of coral and mud dominated the village, and off-shore a narrow channel running between two reefs provided access to the open sea. Another channel to the west of the village was only navigable at spring tide and could be quickly blocked with stones to foil pursuers.

Secure in his base, Rahmah began to terrorize the Gulf's shipping. He differed from other pirates in one important respect: he was very careful in his choice of victims. Rahmah reserved his attention almost exclusively for the Al Khalifa of Bahrain, for whom he nursed an implacable hatred, and for anyone who assisted them. This was to remain the guiding principle to the end of his life, and like all obsessions it contained both accidental advantages and the seeds of his eventual destruction. He always, for instance, scrupulously respected British shipping. On one occasion, when he discovered that the boat he had boarded was carrying horses belonging to the East India Company, he immediately arranged for them to be sent on to Bombay where in time they arrived safely. This policy, though obviously dictated by expedience rather than generosity, served him well. It was one reason why the British expedition sent against the pirates of the Gulf in 1809 left him alone (though the difficulty of mounting a successful attack on Khor Hassan was another factor).

The same unswerving hostility to the Al Khalifa led Rahmah to ally himself with any power opposed to them. This required some quick-footed political manoeuvres on his part, since Bahrain was constantly being threatened

Old Wakrah

Old Wakrah

by invasion from several different directions. Both Persia and Oman claimed the islands, but the most serious challenge to the independence of Bahrain came from the Wahabis who were then sweeping all before them from one side of Arabia to the other. Wahabism was born in the depths of the Arabian desert in the middle of the eighteenth century and was at first a purely religious movement designed to lead the faithful back to the original simplicity of Islam. The new doctrine was taken up by Ibn Saud, the ruler of the central province of Nejd, who proceeded to impose it on his neighbours with such success that his rule soon extended from the Red Sea to the Arabian Gulf.

On her own, Bahrain was no match for the other powers in the Gulf, and for some years the islands became a shuttlecock tossed back and forth between rival aggressors. In 1800, and again two years later, they were briefly occupied by the Sultan of Muscat and Oman, from whom the Al Khalifa took refuge in Zubara. Watching events from his lair in Khor Hassan, Rahmah astutely threw in his lot with the Wahabis, and when they ousted the Sultan from Bahrain, his ambitions, centred as always on the humiliation of the Al Khalifa, began to bear fruit. By 1809 the Wahabis controlled Qatar, and as reward for his services Rahmah was presented with Zubara. The following year, Bahrain, Qatar and Qatif on the mainland were all brought under the rule of a Wahabi governor based in Bahrain. It seemed as if Rahmah's day had come, and he celebrated with a series of spectacular piracies, including the capture of eighteen loaded ships belonging to the Al Khalifa.

But as was to happen more than once in his fluctuating career, Rahmah was denied victory at the very moment when it seemed assured. The reversal of his fortunes came about through the temporary eclipse of the Wahabis. By 1810 the

Turkish Caliphate had become alarmed by the successes of Ibn Saud, who was nominally their vassal. They were in no position, however, to move against him, and the task was left to another Turkish subject, Muhammad Ali, the Pasha of Egypt. In 1811 Ali set out to recover the Red Sea provinces, including the sacred cities of Mecca and Medina, and the effect of these operations was immediately felt in the Gulf. The Sultan of Muscat and Oman, who still harboured designs on Bahrain, seized the opportunity to attack the Wahabis in Qatar. Zubara was burnt to the ground and shortly afterwards the Wahabis withdrew. The Al Khalifa, meanwhile, defeated Rahmah in a fierce naval battle and drove him out of Khor Hassan, forcing him to settle in a new base at Damman on the mainland opposite Bahrain.

Five years later, in the game of musical chairs which the shifting alliances in the Gulf had come to resemble, new groupings were formed. Bahrain was lined up with the Wahabis against Persia and the Sultan of Muscat and Oman. Gravitating as ever to the Al Khalifa's enemy of the day, Rahmah joined the Sultan, thus exactly reversing the coalition of 1811. But once again he had backed the wrong horse. In the battle which followed, the Sultan was decisively defeated. Rahmah's fort at Damman was blown up by the Wahabis, and in October 1816 he arrived at Bushire on the other side of the Gulf as an exile and refugee accompanied by 500 families. It must have been an acutely disappointing moment for the ageing pirate, since the Sultan had promised to install him in Bahrain in place of the Al Khalifa sheikhs if the attack succeeded.

After 1816 Rahmah played little part in the affairs of Qatar, but since he remains a legend in the peninsula to this day, it is worth noting his last exploits, and in particular the dramatic

Old Fort

manner of his death. For two years he stayed in Bushire and then moved back to Damman. His hatred of the Al Khalifa was as strong as ever, and on several occasions he attempted to persuade both the Persians and the Sultan of Muscat and Oman to launch fresh expeditions against Bahrain. But his luck, and his resources, were running out. Rahmah was now almost seventy and completely blind. His fleet was reduced to a single vessel manned by a few surviving followers. When the Al Khalifa laid siege to his fortress at Damman in 1826, his frantic attempts to drum up support from former allies were ignored. Rahmah was now on his own. But as one might have expected, he faced up to the final battle with the same contempt for his enemies that he had displayed all his life. Returning to Damman, he ordered his ship to fire a salute by way of an insult to the waiting Al Khalifa fleet. This so infuriated one Bahraini sheikh that he promptly offered to take Rahmah on in single combat. The offer was accepted and the vessels were soon joined in a ferocious struggle. At one point the Bahraini ship was forced to disengage from the action to pick up reinforcements. Some weeks later, Lieutenant Samuel Hennell, the assistant British Resident in the Gulf, described how it had ended according to reports he received from eye-witnesses:

'Weakened as his crew was in the former combat, Rahmah soon found that he was in no condition to carry on the engagement, and that in a short time he must be taken by boarding, unless he surrendered – an alternative which was out of the question, considering the atrocious and sanguinary warfare he had so long carried on against Bahrain. Having, therefore, given orders for his vessel to grapple with the enemy, he took his youngest son (a fine boy about eight years old) in his arms, and seizing a lighted match, directed his attendants to lead him down to the magazine. Although acquainted with the determined character of their chief, and of course aware of the inevitable destruction which awaited them, his commands were instantly obeyed, and in a few seconds the sea was covered with the scattered timbers of the exploded vessel, and the miserable remains of Rahmah-bin-Jaubir and his devoted followers.'

It was a fitting end to an extraordinary career.

Qatar and the Trucial System

After the departure of Rahmah bin Jabir from the scene, whenever trouble broke out in Doha or one of the villages of the east coast it was automatically assumed to be the responsibility of the Ruler in Bahrain. This, at any rate, was the theory. In practice, the peninsula remained very much a no-man's-land, and it was only along the north-west coast around Zubara that the Al Khalifa exercised any real control. Nevertheless, for the next forty years the history of Qatar is inextricably bound up with events in Bahrain.

Qatar played little part in these events except as a backdrop, a convenient refuge for those who occasionally needed to escape from the centre of the stage. The Al Khalifa sometimes retired there when their homes were threatened, or used it as an outpost from which they could keep a watch on the movements of the Wahabis. It was also a sanctuary for pirates, who had now become a major target for the British.

Several attempts had already been made by the British to deal with the pirate menace, the most notable being the naval expedition of 1809 from which Rahmah bin Jabir was exempted. But the effects had been short-lived, and soon the pirates were once again taking a heavy toll of the shipping in the Gulf. Bahrain became a thriving market for stolen goods, and the only check on the activities of the pirates was the Sultan of Muscat's modest navy. The British watched the growing anarchy at sea uneasily. Their over-riding concern was to protect the route to India. They had no wish to become embroiled in the squabbles and rivalries of the Arab states. But as the sole European power active in the Gulf at the time, they alone had the resources to suppress the pirates. Affairs in the Gulf were controlled by the government in Bombay through the Political Resident in Bushire, and when the pirates began to prey on British vessels, it was decided in India that the time had come to act.

In November 1819, an expedition consisting of nine warships and 3,000 soldiers sailed from India for the Gulf. Off Ras al Khaimah, the pirates' base, they were joined by the Sultan of Muscat with two ships and 600 men. On 3 December the combined force made a landing and captured the town with little difficulty. The pirates' boats were burnt, and the fleet then moved on to visit other ports along the coast.

This decisive action was followed by a General Treaty of Peace signed by all the Arab sheikhs of the Pirate Coast on or soon after 8 January 1820. Under the terms of the treaty, the sheikhs agreed to abstain from plunder and piracy. An important distinction was also made between piracy and lawful warfare. It was a turning point in the history of the Gulf, the first in a series of measures which were eventually to bring peace and order to the sea.

Some time elapsed before the treaty began to work. Securing an agreement was one thing; making it effective was quite another, and in this respect Qatar proved a difficult obstacle. The local people, particularly on the east coast, did much as they pleased, and they were often joined by refugees from other states who resided there in temporary exile. These interlopers constantly threatened the peace by using Qatar as a base from which to launch attacks against their rivals at home.

Restless exiles were not the only problem. The little fishing villages up and down the east coast of the peninsula contained a whole nest of trouble-makers whose activities provoked sporadic retribution from the British or the Bahraini sheikhs. Only a year after the Treaty of Peace, the town of Doha was completely destroyed by the East India Company's cruiser, *Vestal*, on account of several piracies committed by the inhabitants. Two years later, Lieutenant John Macleod, the British Resident in the Gulf,

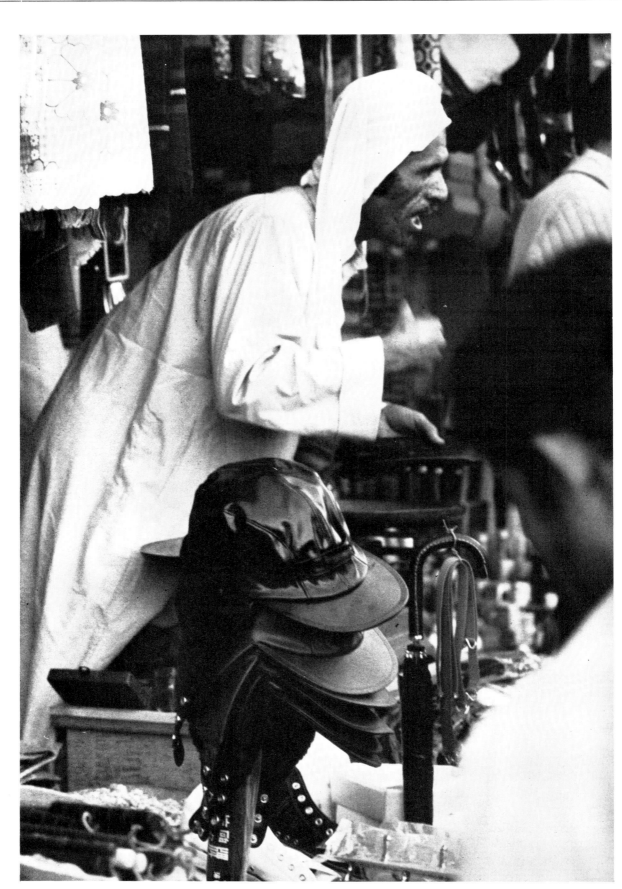

Market Place, Doha

A Qatari face

Bedouin boy

Bedouin boy

Bedouin boy

Young Qataris

Bedouin

Young Qataris

A face from Qatar

Repairing nets

visited Doha and found the citizens largely ignorant of the terms of the treaty. Whether this was true or not, there is no doubt that among them there lived some of the most resourceful pirates of the day.

These free-booting characters operated all over the Gulf and were often able to escape arrest by returning to their havens in Qatar. The village of Fuwairet in the north was known to be the base of a celebrated pirate called Hasum, while Doha harboured an even more notorious individual, Obaid bin Mahanna. A remarkable degree of good luck seems to have accompanied Obaid in his exploits. He was eventually caught on the Persian side of the Gulf by some fishermen whose suspicions were aroused when he inquired about a small boat anchored in the local harbour. But on being handed over to the British Resident in Bushire, he was miraculously saved from the gallows by a sudden outbreak of political revolution in the town, during which he was able to make his escape.

Elsewhere in the Gulf the pirates were less active after 1820. But one major flaw in the treaty soon became apparent. The Arab sheikhdoms were bound to refrain from piracy; but they were not prevented from indulging in 'legitimate' warfare. Over the years, quarrelling with one's neighbour had become almost a way of life in the Gulf. Since these squabbles were outside the scope of the treaty, they continued unabated. And, inevitably, 'legitimate' warfare was often a cover for piracy. These disturbances, apart from threatening the local shipping, were a serious hazard to pearl-diving operations. Clearly, if peace were to mean anything in the Gulf, a new and more far-reaching treaty would have to be arranged. Somewhat surprisingly, this was achieved in 1835 when Captain Hennell, the same man who had reported the death of Rahmah bin Jabir, inaugurated the First Maritime Truce. The truce outlawed all warfare between 21 May and 21 November, the period of the pearl-diving season. It was from this date that the sheikhdoms east of Qatar came to be known as the 'Trucial' rather than the 'Pirate' Coast. The truce was renewed annually until 1843, when it was extended for a further ten years. Finally, in 1853, it was made permanent.

Curiously enough, Bahrain was excluded from the agreements. There were two reasons: first, Bahrain had never been one of the pirate strongholds; and, more importantly, the British feared that if the Sultan of Muscat threatened to invade the islands again, the Bahraini sheikhs would solicit their help – a prospect which was bound to embarrass the British, given their policy of not interfering in local disputes. One inevitable result of Bahrain's exclusion from the trucial system was that Qatar also was left out, and thus continued to be a haven for trouble-makers. In the very year that the First Maritime Truce was signed, a colony of Bani Yas exiles from Abu Dhabi established themselves in Khor al Odeid, a remote part of the east coast on the neck of the peninsula. From here they sallied out to harass passing vessels. They were aided and abetted in these ventures by the local villages, who supplied them with water and provisions until the British decided to intervene. Two sloops of war and a schooner visited Doha and Wakrah in 1836 and persuaded the head sheikhs to take action against the Bani Yas. But for some years to come Qatar continued to be one of the last remaining pirate strongholds in the Gulf.

Civil War in Bahrain

While piracy was gradually being brought under control, a new threat to the peace of the Gulf emerged in the shape of a civil war in Bahrain, in which Qatar was to be one of the main theatres of action. By 1835, Bahrain was beginning to slip into anarchy. Sheikh Abdulla bin Ahmed had been in power for nearly forty years, sharing his rule first with his brother Salman, who died in 1825, and then with Salman's son Khalifa, who in turn died in 1834. Left on his own, Sheikh Abdulla presided over a government which was arbitrary, feeble and corrupt. His own sons openly defied his authority with bands of armed followers sometimes numbering several hundred men. The towns fell into ruins, trade declined by half and a steady exodus of people was slowly depopulating the islands.

Even in Qatar, Abdulla's authority was being challenged. The first serious revolt broke out in 1835 at the village of Huwailah on the north-east coast. Angered by the Bahraini Ruler's extortionate demands on them, the Al bin Ali tribe, who lived in Huwailah, appealed for help to the Wahabis through one of Abdulla's rebellious sons. Several ships belonging to Bahrain were attacked, but after a while the two parties negotiated a truce in which it was agreed that the village should be evacuated, and the Al bin Ali moved to Bahrain. Almost immediately the truce was broken by Abdulla, who instigated an assault on Huwailah in which a ship was sunk.

Sheikh Abdulla's problems continued to multiply. At one stage he threatened to escape from his troublesome relatives in Bahrain by moving to Qatar. In fact he went so far as to send two of his wives with their families, furniture and even the doors of their houses to Khor Hassan, Rahmah bin Jabir's old haunt.

Before he could follow them, he found he had a revolt on his hands in Bahrain led by his great-nephew, Sheikh Muhammad bin Khalifa. In keeping with such quarrels, the immediate cause was trivial: Muhammad had tried to prevent a young Bahraini girl from marrying Abdulla's son Ahmed. The old sheikh resented his interference, and soon the two sides began recruiting Bedouin from the mainland, whose readiness to enlist sprang from promises held out to them of plunder. Most of Muhammad's support came from Qatar, but Abdulla held the initiative in Bahrain and in 1842 succeeded in driving his rival out of the islands. He then moved over to the mainland and allowed his Bedouin followers to sack Khor Hassan while he himself started to rebuild Zubara, which had been abandoned for over thirty years.

It proved to be a Pyrrhic victory. Already Muhammad was regrouping, and by the following year he had assembled a motley alliance of familiar figures, among them Bashir bin Rahmah, a son of the great pirate. The combined forces of the allies were based at Fuwairet, and from there, in the spring of 1843, they mounted an all-out assault on Bahrain. The battle did not last long. Finding himself outnumbered, Abdulla capitulated and was allowed to depart with his family and possessions packed into two small boats.

The struggle was not yet over, however. In 1847 the two sides met in a battle near Fuwairet and this time it was to prove decisive. Leading his troops in person, Muhammed inflicted a severe defeat on his great-uncle.

After this protracted conflict a lull settled over the peninsula, and, apart from one incident, nothing much happened in Qatar for the next twenty years. The solitary event of importance was the visit of the Wahabi Amir Feisal, who in 1851 came to within two days' march of Doha. During the Bahrain civil war, the Wahabis waited in the wings, favouring Muhammad's cause on the whole, but constantly threatening to take over Bahrain. As in the past, the Bahraini

sheikhs had from time to time taken the precaution of paying nominal tribute to gain the Wahabis' goodwill.

Now, on the Amir's arrival in Qatar, the main towns along the east coast, including Doha, Wakharah and Fuwairet, decided to repudiate their allegiance to Bahrain and join the Wahabis. Sheikh Muhammad's attempt to prevent this happening nearly lost him the whole peninsula, and he was only saved by British intervention. In the settlement which followed, Doha and the other towns were returned to Bahrain and

Muhammad agreed to pay annual tribute to the Wahabis. The nature of this tribute is interesting, since it established Qatar's status at the time. Colonel Lewis Pelly, the Resident in the Gulf, decided that it was paid by Bahrain, not on its own account, but as a form of protection money to secure Bahrain's subjects in Qatar against aggression from Wahabi tribes on the mainland. This interpretation was significant in view of the dramatic and far-reaching events which were about to overtake the peninsula.

1867: The Great Attack on Qatar

Eighteen sixty-seven was to be a traumatic year for the people of Qatar, but few of them can have guessed what was in store as they calmly prepared for the pearling season. The first hint of trouble came when a Bedouin from the peninsula was suddenly seized and deported to Bahrain. The tribal chieftains of Qatar immediately demanded his release, and when this was refused, prepared to eject Sheikh Muhammad's representative from Wakrah. Before they could act, however, this individual prudently withdrew to Khor Hassan on the other side of the peninsula. A reconciliation then took place: the Bedouin was returned and the Qatari sheikhs apologized for their behaviour to the Bahraini Ruler. One of them, Sheikh Jasim bin Muhammad al Thani, accepted an invitation to visit Bahrain to discuss arrangements for the future administration of the peninsula. It appeared that the affair had been settled to the satisfaction of all parties until news reached Qatar that Sheikh Jasim had been flung into prison. Only then did the devious intentions of the Bahraini Ruler become apparent. For he immediately dispatched an expedition of twenty-four boats with 500 men under the command of his brother, Sheikh Ali, against the people of Doha and Wakrah. At the same time, he appealed for help to the rulers of Dubai and Abu Dhabi. Sheikh Zaid of Abu Dhabi was then the most powerful man on the Trucial Coast, and he was able to raise a force of 2,000 men in seventy boats in response to Bahrain's appeal. Arriving first, the Abu Dhabi contingent waited off the Qatar coast, where it was eventually joined by the Bahraini fleet. The allies then fell upon the defenceless towns and plundered them with such ferocity that even the rafters and doors of houses were removed. Some of the inhabitants were deported, others were ordered to settle elsewhere and robbed of their possessions as they left. When it was all over, the aggressors sailed away with £50,000-worth of booty.

Nothing like this had happened in the Gulf for over thirty years. It was the most flagrant breach of the peace since the First Maritime Truce had been signed in 1835, and the British were immediately aware that the attack was a direct challenge to the whole trucial system. Bahrain could no longer plead that she was not a party to these agreements. Some years before, the continuing threats to the sheikhdom had forced Britain to modify her policy of non-intervention. At one time, both the Persians and the Turks had sent agents to Bahrain, and a comical display had ensued in which the respective flags of each country were alternately hoisted and lowered over the islands. This was enough for the British, who decided that the independence of Bahrain was essential for maintaining the maritime peace. In 1861 they signed a convention with Sheikh Muhammad on much the same lines as the agreements with the other Trucial States. Now, six years later, Bahrain had blatantly ignored her obligations, and all along the Trucial Coast the Arab sheikhs were waiting and watching to see whether she would get away with it. Characteristically, the British were chronically unprepared to deal with the crisis. The only warship in the Gulf was the *Hugh Rose*, a gunboat manned entirely by Indians and unable to steam for more than eight hours at a time. The s.s. *Sind* was sent to join the *Hugh Rose*, but because of a remarkable oversight arrived from India without any shot for her guns. A few years previously, the Royal Navy had taken over the role of the old Indian Navy in the Gulf, and this to some extent explained the chaotic situation. At all events, Colonel Lewis Pelly had to confine his immediate actions to letters of remonstration addressed to the aggressors. Both sheikhs responded defiantly, particu-

larly the Ruler of Bahrain, who claimed that he had every right to punish those he regarded as his recalcitrant subjects.

But before anything further could be done, the outraged inhabitants of Doha and Wakrah took matters into their own hands. Having waited in vain for the British to act, they now decided to exact their revenge by attacking Bahrain. A fleet was assembled and in June 1868 a bloody but inconclusive engagement took place off the north coast of Qatar in which sixty ships and 1,000 men were lost. The situation was now getting out of hand, but still the British were waiting for reinforcements. Not until the beginning of September could Colonel Pelly sail for Bahrain with a small fleet which included the *Sind*, armed at last with shot for its guns. At Bahrain they found Sheikh Muhammad had already fled. Colonel Pelly promptly announced that Muhammad had forfeited the sheikhdom and installed his brother Ali in his place. On 6 September Ali signed an agreement by which he promised to pay £20,000 compensation to the people of Doha and Wakrah; he was also compelled to burn all his warships. A fifth of the money was collected immediately, but the remainder was remitted.

After leaving Bahrain, Colonel Pelly sailed on to Qatar. As soon as he arrived in Wakrah he summoned the local sheikhs on board. Among them was Muhammad bin Thani, the father of Jasim, whose imprisonment in Bahrain had caused all the trouble. By now Pelly had realized that the Al Thanis were the most powerful family in Qatar. According to tradition, they had migrated from Central Arabia to the Jibrin oasis, 150 miles inland from the peninsula, during the late seventeenth century. From there they had moved by stages to Ruwais, Zubara and Fuwairet before finally settling at Doha.

It was with Muhammad bin Thani that Colonel Pelly negotiated the important treaty of 12 September 1868. Its terms were similar to the other trucial pacts. Muhammad agreed, among other things, not to make war at sea and to refer any disputes to the British Resident. He also promised to maintain his family's traditional relationship with the new Sheikh of Bahrain, and to allow the British to settle any problems which arose regarding the question of tribute. In a supplementary treaty signed a few months later, the amount due was fixed at £400 a year.

Before leaving Wakrah, Pelly managed to extract compensation from some of the local inhabitants who had robbed a British subject. The fine was paid partly in cash and partly in the form of a bill to be paid by a wealthy pearl merchant living on the Persian coast; the bill was secured by a sealed bag of pearls handed over to Pelly for him to deliver to the merchant on receipt of payment.

Thus ended a year which turned out to be a landmark in Qatar's history. For the first time the affairs of the peninsula were in the hands of the local people. From that date, Bahrain, though continuing for a while to receive tribute from the mainland, no longer laid any serious claim to Qatar except for the sea around Zubara. The rest of the country fell increasingly under the influence of the Al Thani family, who have ruled it ever since. But in 1868 the country was still not free from the threat of foreign interference, and there were plenty of candidates waiting to fill the vacuum left by Bahrain's withdrawal.

Grand Mosque, Doha

Sunset, Old Fort

Museum of Development, Doha

Museum of Development, Doha

Doors

Old Wakrah

Door

Hunting lodge

Painted doorway, Wakrah

Old mosque, Old Wakrah

Museum of Development, Doha

Old mosque, Old Wakrah

Palgrave's Visit to Qatar

A few years before these events, the English traveller, William Palgrave, had visited Qatar in the course of his epic journey across Arabia. Some idea of what the place was like at the time and how the people lived emerges from the account he left of his brief stay there. Palgrave arrived in Doha by boat from Bahrain on 29 January 1863. His first impressions were not particularly favourable:

'To have an idea of Katar, my readers must figure to themselves miles on miles of low barren hills, bleak and sun-scorched, with hardly a single tree to vary their dry monotonous outline: below these a muddy beach extends for a quarter of a mile seaward in slimy quicksands, bordered by a ridge of sludge and seaweed.'

Palgrave's visit lasted ten days, during which time he was the guest of Muhammad bin Thani, whom he described as 'a shrewd wary old man, slightly corpulent, and renowned for prudence and good-humoured easiness of demeanour, but close-fisted and a hard customer at a bargain'. Muhammad told Palgrave how they survived in Qatar:

' "We are all from the highest to the lowest slaves of one master, Pearl," said to me one evening Mohammed-ebn-Thanee, chief of Bedaa; nor was the expression out of place. All thought, all conversation, all employment, turns on that one subject; everything else is mere by-game, and below even secondary consideration.'

He was not exaggerating. By the time Palgrave arrived in Qatar, European competition and the restrictions imposed by the foreigners on local traders had deprived the Arabs of their alternative sources of wealth. The slave trade was forbidden and piracy had ceased to be a profitable enterprise. Nor were the Arab dhows any match for European ships in carrying coffee, cloth and sugar on the Indian trade route. The first steamer had appeared in the Gulf in 1838, and twenty-five years later there was a regular service between Bombay and Basra.

All that was left to the Arabs were the pearls and fishes of the sea. No wonder they had a belief that a pearl was a drop of dew or rain which the oyster took in by rising to the surface of the sea at night or during a shower. At least the pearl trade had benefited by the efforts of the British to bring peace to the area. By the middle of the nineteenth century, more than 50,000 men and 2,000 boats were engaged in the trade, and the value of the catch was usually around £400,000 a year. What Qatar's share was is not recorded, but to judge from Palgrave's observations it must have been considerable, particularly as the richest pearl beds were off Ras Rakan, the northern tip of the peninsula.

To these banks and others along the coast a flotilla of boats sailed out every May at the beginning of the pearling season. At first they had no compasses or charts and captains relied on the stars to guide them in their destination. The crews of the boats ranged from ten to forty, and they remained on the pearl banks all summer. Diving continued from sunrise to sunset. The day started with a breakfast of coffee and dates, and then the divers worked until nightfall with a half-hour break for lunch. Their equipment was very simple: a clip on the nose, plugs in their ears, pads to protect their fingers from cuts and a bag hung round their neck to put the oysters in. Sometimes they wore a long white shirt to protect themselves from the deadly sting of the devil fish; against sharks there was little they could do. During a day's work a diver might make as many as fifty plunges, sometimes reaching a depth of twelve fathoms. It was a very tough life and the rewards were meagre. Most of the profits went to the merchants who, from time to time, sailed out to the banks and collected the pearls, which were sold in the markets of Bahrain.

During the summer months the villages along the coastline were almost deserted, and each community employed a watchman to warn against attack. A special tax was levied on the pearl fleets to pay for the services of these watchmen. When they gave the alarm, a message was sent to the pearl banks and the men would hurry back to protect their villages. In the meantime, their families withdrew to the 'towers of refuge' which Palgrave noticed during his visit:

'They are small circular buildings from twenty-five to thirty feet in height, each with a door about half-way up the side and a rope hanging out; by this compendious ladder the Katar shepherds, when scared by a sudden attack, clamber up for safety into the interior of the tower, and once there draw in the rope after them, thus securing their own lives and persons at any rate, whatever may become of their cattle.'

These raids were invariably carried out by the Bedouin, who visited the peninsula at various times of the year. The range of a nomadic tribe is known as a *dirrah* and extends for several hundred miles. Qatar formed part of the *dirrah* of four different tribes. The Bani Hajir and the Manasir wandered between the peninsula and the Trucial Coast. The Al Morra came south from Hasa. The Naim had broken off from an Omani tribe and now divided their time between Bahrain and Qatar. Some of these tribes came peacefully, others could be very hostile. The Bani Hajir, for instance, were partial to piracy, and the Al Morra were always on the look-out for plunder. The Naim, on the other hand, often joined the pearl fleet, while the Manasir came to the peninsula in the winter to pasture their camels and sheep, retiring in the summer to the Liwa oasis on the edge of the Empty Quarter where they harvested dates. Although they were frequently elsewhere, the tribes were an important force in the internal affairs of the country. They regarded themselves as independent of all authority, but were, in fact, usually under the protection of one of the local sheikhs. The Bani Hajir generally gave their allegiance to the Al Thani family, while the Naim supported the rulers of Bahrain. These alliances were never permanent, and a tribe might suddenly switch its loyalty from one sheikh to another depending on the strength of his position. It was the Al Thanis' skilful handling of the Bedouin, as much as any other factor, which enabled them to rule the country from 1868 onwards.

Sheikh Jasim and the Turkish Occupation

For several years after the great attack on Qatar, everything was quiet in the peninsula. The feuds of the Bahraini sheikhs had been resolved, and with the new agreement signed by Muhammad bin Thani, it looked as though the country would gradually be drawn into the trucial system. Events in the Gulf, however, had seldom been predictable. There were too many rival powers in the area, and despite the growing British naval presence, any one of them was liable to disrupt the peace at any moment. On this occasion it was the arrival of Turkey on the scene which suddenly changed the picture. The Ottoman Empire had been disintegrating for some time. In an attempt to arrest, or at least divert attention from what was happening, the Turks decided to embark on a policy of territorial expansion in Arabia. The opportunity arose when a quarrel broke out between Abdulla and Sauc, the sons of the great Wahabi Amir, Faisal bin Turki. When Abdulla appealed for help to the Turks, they responded swiftly. In July 1871 a Turkish expedition occupied the province of Hasa, and within a few days a delegation turned up in Doha demanding that the Al Thanis should acknowledge Turkish sovereignty.

These events soon reached the ears of the British Resident, who immediately dispatched his assistant, Major Sidney Smith, to discover what was going on. On arriving in Doha, Smith found the Turkish flag flying over the town. From Muhammad bin Thani he heard what had happened. A Kuwaiti go-between had apparently tried to persuade Muhammad to become a vassal of the Ottoman Empire, but the old sheikh had refused. He had resolutely continued to fly the Arab flag over his own house, and it was his son, Sheikh Jasim, who had allowed the Turkish flag to be raised. When the British protested to the authorities in Baghdad, they were told that Turkish assurances to respect

the independence of the Gulf states had not covered Qatar.

Such were the haphazard circumstances in which the Turkish occupation of the peninsula began. Although they were to remain there forty years, their presence was for the most part passive. The Turkish garrison which was installed in Doha never numbered more than a few hundred men, and the affairs of the country outside the town continued to be controlled by the Al Thanis. Nevertheless, the arrival of the Turks had several important repercussions. It removed from Qatar for the time being the threat of other invaders. It also inevitably aroused the deepest suspicions of the British, who feared, with some justification, that the Turks would use Qatar as a springboard to invade Bahrain and extend their influence further east to the Trucial States. Through diplomatic channels, the British made it quite clear that they did not recognize Turkish rights in Qatar; yet they tacitly accepted their presence in Doha, and tried to avoid doing anything which would allow them to assert their claims.

What concerned the British more was the sudden increase in piracy and general disorder which took place as soon as the Turks appeared on the scene, and which they saw as a threat to the whole trucial system. This preoccupation was a source of endless protests and counter-protests between the two countries, most of which came to nothing.

In the middle of these two interloping powers, and dominating the affairs of Qatar for almost as long as the Turkish occupation, was the redoubtable figure of Sheikh Jasim, Muhammad bin Thani's son. When the Turks arrived, Jasim was already the most influential person in the peninsula, and after his father died in 1878, his pre-eminence among the local sheikhs was unquestioned. His chief objective was to keep

48

49

his country independent from outside forces, and this he did with consummate skill, playing off one party against another. When the British chastised him, he invoked the aid of the Turks; when the Turks became oppressive, he looked for help to the British; and when he fell out with both parties, he withdrew disdainfully into the desert, disclaiming all responsibility for what might happen in his absence.

At the same time, Jasim had to contend with various neighbouring sheikhs who disputed his jurisdiction over parts of the peninsula. In the north the Al Khalifa still controlled the area around Zubara. It was partly in the hope of removing them that Jasim had originally welcomed the Turks in Doha; and the same motive led him to ally himself with Nasir bin Muburak, a political exile who had accompanied Sheikh Muhammad, the deposed Ruler of Bahrain, when he invaded the islands in 1869. At the other end of the peninsula, at Khor al Odeid, Jasim was involved in a running quarrel with Sheikh Zaid of Abu Dhabi over a group of Bani Yas colonists. In both these affairs, and in all his dealings with the various people who interfered with his ambitions, Jasim revealed himself as shrewd and determined, a man whom his adversaries could never quite outwit.

In the autumn of 1871, however, Jasim was an unknown quantity and the Turks must have been delighted with the reception he gave them. For his part, Jasim saw the Turks as a useful ally against other interfering powers. Already they had been of service. For several months after the Turkish occupation of Hasa, hordes of Bedouin tribesmen used Qatar as a base to harass the invaders. At one point the Wahabi Amir, Saud, had settled in the peninsula and compelled the local people to furnish him with supplies. Making use of his new connections, Jasim appealed to the Turks and was gratified when no less a person

than Midhat Pasha, the Wali of Baghdad, came immediately and cleared the Bedouin out. In January 1872 a hundred Turkish troops with a field gun arrived in Doha and established a base in one of the town's forts. The occupation was complete.

It was not long, however, before disenchantment set in. Jasim soon found the presence of the Turks in Doha more irritating than the British ships which kept a watchful eye on his activities at sea. The Turkish representative insisted on being consulted on even the most trivial matter, and made constant demands for money to pay for the upkeep of the garrison. The appointment of Jasim as Governor of Qatar in 1879 failed to win him over, and it was only fear of being deported to Constantinople that secured his grudging collaboration.

Jasim's relations with the British were equally strained. His reluctance to do anything to suppress the wave of piracy which had broken out around Qatar's coastline was partly to blame. The trouble from the British point of view was that the Turkish presence in Doha made it difficult to punish piracies committed around the coasts of Qatar; it also put the 1868 agreement with the Al Thani sheikhs in some doubt. Jasim continued to defer to the British in matters affecting maritime law and order, but he knew he could always take refuge from their sanctions by appealing to the Turks. He was even prepared to plead with the British that he did not possess sufficient power to control his subjects outside Doha and Wakrah, and in 1881 he wrote somewhat disingenuously to the British Resident:

'The El Katr coast is very large and extensive with many ports, and I have not the power to forbid [anyone from landing or embarking] . . . unless you give strict orders to all people . . . to migrate and settle in my country and be subject to me.'

This, of course, was impossible, and the British merely contented themselves with making Jasim promise that he would abide by the terms of the 1868 agreement.

Another source of friction between the British and the Al Thani sheikh was his continual harassment of Indian pearl traders in Doha who were British subjects. Jasim resented their competition, and in 1882 closed their shops and expelled them from the town. This brought an instant response from the British Resident, who sailed to Doha and forced him to pay compensation and allow the Indians to return. Characteristically, Jasim appealed to the Turks and threatened to resign his position as Governor of Qatar unless they refunded him the money. And, almost immediately, he renewed his campaign against the Indians. Changing his tactics, Jasim left Doha, loudly proclaiming that he was not responsible for anything that might happen while he was away. A group of Bani Hajir then attacked the Indians, wounding two of them slightly. The final outcome of these petty squabbles was the withdrawal of all the Indians from Doha and the appropriation of some pearls held by Jasim in Bahrain by way of compensation.

While all this was going on in Doha, events of a more dramatic character were taking place in the north of the peninsula. The Bahrainis still controlled Zubara through their close allies, the Naim. The tribe moved freely between the islands and the mainland, and many of them had enlisted in the bodyguard of Sheikh Isa bin Ali, the Ruler of Bahrain. In Zubara their position was made uneasy by the occasional presence in Qatar of the Al Khalifa's most bitter enemy, Nasir bin Mubarak. For some time Nasir had unsuccessfully tried to persuade the British to intercede on his behalf for the return of his properties in Bahrain. Next he turned to the Turks, who were more accommodating. Seeing

him as a useful instrument for promoting their own designs on Bahrain, they paid him an annual allowance. At the same time he gained the favour of Sheikh Jasim, who, apart from being his father-in-law, also hoped to profit from Nasir's machinations against the Al Khalifa.

Not surprisingly, the Bahraini sheikhs were alarmed by this hostile build-up across the water. When their urgent requests to establish a garrison at Zubara were turned down by the British, the stage was set for the first of several attempted invasions, both real and imaginary, which were to menace Bahrain during the next twenty years. The signal that something was afoot came in August 1874 when 300 or 400 Bani Hajir tribesmen, led by relations of Nasir, collected on the Qatar coast and tried to find some boats to take them over to Bahrain. Their intentions were frustrated by the presence of several British warships in the area, so the Bani Hajir turned instead on the Naim and besieged them in their fort at Zubara. Many of the Naim were away on the pearl banks at the time, and it was only when they made a sudden reappearance that the attackers were driven off with heavy losses.

After this scare, the British attempted to restrain the Sheikh of Bahrain from becoming involved in affairs on the mainland, and they summarily rejected a claim he made in 1875 to sovereignty over the whole of Qatar. Trouble, however, continued in Zubara. A particularly brutal piracy committed by the Naim in September 1878 provoked retaliation from a large force led by Sheikh Jasim and Nasir. Hearing of the conflict, Colonel E.C. Ross, the British Resident, hurried to the scene, and on 18 November visited Jasim in his camp. He found him surrounded by about 2,000 armed men half a mile from the fort of Murair in which 500 Naim were besieged. The village of Zubara had already been completely

Old mosque, Old **Wakrah**

Old Wakrah

destroyed. Shortly after Ross's departure, the Naim surrendered. Some of them emigrated to Bahrain, while others accompanied Jasim back to Doha, and from then on Zubara ceased to exist.

Two years later rumours reached the British Resident that Nasir bin Mubarak was once again on the move, this time riding with a strong Bedouin force towards the villages of Ruwais and Abu Dhuluf on the northern tip of Qatar. H.M.S. *Beacon* was sent to reconnoitre the coast, but found everything quiet. Two days after she had sailed away, Nasir emerged from the desert and ordered the villagers to hand over their boats. But he was too late: warned of his intentions, they had already moved them elsewhere.

Unable to achieve his aims by force, Nasir returned to making appeals to the British for the restitution of his property in Bahrain. As usual they were refused, and in 1881 Jasim was warned that from now on he would be held responsible for Nasir's conduct. Jasim was, in fact, already beginning to tire of his ally. The prospect of incurring the wrath of the British on Nasir's account merely diminished his enthusiasm for his son-in-law's cause. For the next ten years no serious attempts were made on Bahrain, although once or twice rumours of invasion set off panic in the islands. Otherwise relations between the Al Thani and the Al Khalifa were for the moment reasonably friendly. When the Ruler of Bahrain's brother made a hunting expedition to the west coast of Qatar, Jasim even agreed to visit in his camp.

All this time Jasim was engaged in a separate conflict at the other end of the peninsula against the Sheikh of Abu Dhabi. Here the point at issue was the allegiance of a colony of Bani Yas tribesmen who had left Abu Dhabi and settled in Khor al Odeid. This was their third term of exile – they had come to Odeid for brief periods

in 1835 and 1849 – and on each occasion it had caused friction between the rulers of their original and adopted homes. Sheikh Zaid of Abu Dhabi complained that their presence in Odeid threatened the prosperity of his people, while Sheikh Jasim welcomed it as a convenient excuse to extend his authority over the area. At one point the Turks had also shown an interest in the colony. The Bani Yas, for their part, claimed to be independent of all parties, but prudently acquired both a Trucial and a Turkish flag, raising each one as the occasion demanded.

The colony consisted of about 200 tribesmen with their wives and families and thirty pearling boats. When Captain Guthrie, the senior British naval officer in the Gulf, visited it in October 1876, he found the place well defended.

'Its defences consist of a small square fort with two towers, in the centre of the town. On the right is a line of four towers, at some distance from each other, running towards the foot of the hills. Within these again, and near the beach, are two other detached towers, which, with one at the back of the town, complete the defences on the right. The other side is protected only by a sort of square block house, which, situated upon a small elevation, commands the wells from which the place is supplied with water.'

The colony might well have been left undisturbed if Khor al Odeid had not become a refuge for pirates. Whether the Bani Yas themselves were engaged in piracy is uncertain, but the place acquired such a notorious reputation that in 1878 the British, in collusion with the Sheikh of Abu Dhabi, decided to take action. Hearing of these plans, the colonists abandoned Odeid and fled to Doha. Two years later they returned to Abu Dhabi.

Far from settling the dispute, these developments infuriated Sheikh Jasim, who immediately threatened to occupy Odeid. In this enterprise he

was baulked by the British, and there then began a series of spectacular raids and counter-raids between Qatar and Abu Dhabi in which camels, slaves and cattle were carried off by parties of Bedouin on each side. In 1888 the conflict was embittered by the death of one of Sheikh Jasim's sons in an ambush laid by 250 Bedouin a few miles from Doha. Jasim was distraught and appealed for help to all and sundry: the Turks, the Rashids and even the other Trucial States. But all he received were a few tepid expressions of sympathy, and in January of the following year he took his own vicious revenge. At the head of a column of Bedouin, he descended on the Liwa Oasis in the Sheikh of Abu Dhabi's territory, cut down the date plantations and killed everyone in sight, including the women and children. The struggle continued for several years after this with no conclusive result, although Jasim had the best of it on the whole.

The Turks played only a minor role in these affairs. Their troops were instructed to help defend Doha, but they were forbidden to operate at a greater distance than four hours' march from the town. By now their relations with Jasim were deteriorating rapidly. The Al Thani sheikh was incensed by their plan to establish a customs house in Doha. The most effective way to frustrate the project, he considered, was to diminish the importance of the town; and this he did very neatly by withdrawing in 1887 to Dha'ain, a village north of Doha, announcing on his departure that he was no longer responsible for the affairs of Qatar, which would in future be 'first referred to God and then to the Turkish Government'. No sooner had he left than trouble broke out in Doha and the bazaar was plundered by a party of the Bani Hajir.

The Turks responded by strengthening their garrison and establishing a coal depot in the town. But their attempts to mollify Jasim with an offer of a title and decoration were not well received. When the Turkish Governor of Hasa visited Doha in July 1889, he was met by Jasim with a retinue of 600 armed men and a posse of camel riders carrying loaded Martini rifles. The Governor brought with him proposals for reorganizing the administration in Qatar. He suggested that since Jasim was so often absent, an assistant should be appointed to deal with day-to-day affairs. He also proposed that extra taxes should be levied on pearl dealers and other merchants, that a harbour master should be appointed, that Turkish posts should be established at Zubara and Odeid and that cavalry as well as infantry should be stationed in Doha.

Jasim's reaction to these suggestions was immediate: he offered his resignation as Governor of Qatar, and shortly afterwards proclaimed that the administration of the province was now in the hands of Turkish officials. Both parties were rapidly moving towards a showdown. The Bedouin tribes in the peninsula were becoming restless, and hardly a month went by without some murder or robbery taking place. It was in this atmosphere of growing anarchy that matters were suddenly brought to a head by the arrival in Doha of Nafiz Pasha, the Turkish Wali of Basra.

The Wali had been on a tour of the province of Hasa, and travelled on to Qatar with the intention of settling affairs there once and for all. Accompanied by 300 cavalry and a regiment of infantry, he reached Doha towards the end of February 1893 and promptly summoned Jasim to his presence. But Jasim had prudently withdrawn from the town, and despite an offer of safe conduct, refused to move. Instead he suggested that they meet with small escorts in the desert. This was equally unacceptable to Nafiz Pasha, either because he suspected a trick or because he was unwilling to compromise his dignity. Whatever the reason, the position was now one of deadlock. For a whole month the two sides carried on negotiations through the intermediary of Jasim's brother, Sheikh Ahmed, but neither was prepared to budge. At length Nafiz Pasha decided to take the initiative.

Jasim had pitched his camp at Wajbah, a sandy depression about twelve miles west of Doha. It was one of those rare oases in the interior. There were three masonry wells providing good water, and a walled garden which belonged to one of Jasim's sons. Bedouin often visited the wells. Today, over eighty years since that day when the Arabs waited patiently at Wajbah for the Turks to move, the place looks as if it has changed very little. A large fort now dominates the depression, and down in the hollow there is a ruined summer-house full of raised tiled baths surrounded by mosaics. The brick wells have survived, though they are no longer used, and around them an occasional flock of goats grazes on the scrub trees. The Bedouin still come there. Sometimes you can see one of them riding a camel round the depression, a rare sight in Qatar today.

It was here on 26 March 1893 that the first skirmishes took place of a battle which has since become famous in Qatar's history. Having first arrested Sheikh Ahmed and twelve other leading men in Doha, Nafiz Pasha moved out of the town on the night of the 25th. His object was to surprise Jasim in his camp. But the news that the Turks were on their way preceded them, and when they reached Wajbah, Jasim's Bedouins emerged silently from the desert and fell upon their attackers. The Turkish column was scattered and then relentlessly harried as it retreated rapidly back to base. At Misamir, seven miles south of Doha, the fighting was very fierce, and only when they reached the outskirts of the town

did the retiring troops receive some relief from the guns of the Turkish warship *Mirrikh*, anchored in the harbour. Eventually they regained their fort in Doha, and Nafiz Pasha took refuge on the *Mirrikh*.

Jasim's lightly armed Bedouins had suffered heavily in the encounter, and the total Arab casualties, including a large number of people killed in the bombardment of Doha by the Turkish ship, amounted to 400. The Turks only lost 100 men, but had suffered a humiliating defeat. Jasim was able to secure the release of his brother and the other prisoners by seizing the wells near Doha, thus depriving the garrison of water. He also extracted favourable terms from the Turks for allowing the remains of their battered cavalry to return in safety overland to Hasa. In the meantime, the citizens of Doha

abandoned their homes and scattered to other places. Jasim retired to Wajbah, and Nafiz Pasha stayed on board the *Mirrikh* in Doha harbour, anxiously contemplating his future.

For some time after the battle of Wajbah it looked as though the Al Thani sheikhs might rid themselves of the Turks and settle elsewhere under British supervision. Jasim had in fact approached the Political Resident before the battle with a desperate plea for help. He had also, rather surprisingly, asked permission from the Ruler of Bahrain to transfer himself and his followers to the sheikh's territory near Zubara. Naturally the British were very interested in these proposals, and when they heard about the Turkish defeat, an agent was immediately sent to Doha with an offer to mediate. Nafiz Pasha refused to negotiate, however, until he had

received instructions from Constantinople, and in the meantime news arrived of his dismissal. The British agent then went on to visit the Al Thani sheikhs at Wakrah. Here he was told by Ahmed, acting for Jasim, that they would readily accept British arbitration. Once again Ahmed asked that the family be allowed to move to some other part of Qatar. He also announced that they were eager to make an agreement with the British similar to those of the Trucial States. For the moment nothing came of these suggestions, and in June 1893 the Turks finally reached a settlement with the Al Thani brothers. Jasim was given a free pardon and allowed to resign as Governor of Qatar in favour of Ahmed; and in return, the Turks recovered the arms they had lost at the battle of Wajbah.

Sheikh Jasim's Death

The Turks' position in Qatar was severely weakened by their defeat. The garrison had to be strengthened and a Turkish official was appointed assistant governor. But at the same time the uncomfortable partnership with the Al Thani sheikhs was resumed. The Turks refused Jasim's resignation: they probably thought he was less of a menace in an official role than when left to his own devices. It was an uneasy time for them. In 1894 the assistant governor and his wife were murdered by two Turkish soldiers, who fled to Wakrah, where they were arrested. A few years later a minor rebellion broke out in Doha during the temporary absence of the Turkish gunboat which was usually anchored in the port. The cause of the trouble was the belief that the Turks were behind a successful raid made by the Sheikh of Kuwait on the Bani Hajir, who were under Jasim's protection. Arabs as well as Turks were killed in the incident, and the Turkish garrison was once again reinforced.

These domestic problems were insignificant compared with the storm which suddenly blew up in 1895 at that perennial trouble-spot, Zubara. The affair had all the classic ingredients of the confrontations which had taken place there over the previous twenty-five years: a threatened invasion of Bahrain triggered off by split tribal loyalties; the Turks stirring up hostilities in the background; Jasim, as usual, seeking to turn the situation to his own advantage; and the British doggedly defending the independence of Bahrain.

On this occasion, events were set in motion by the emigration from Bahrain to Qatar of the discontented Al bin Ali tribe led by Sheikh Sultan bin Salamah. The tribe were welcomed by Jasim, who invited them to settle on the long-deserted site of Zubara. This suggestion was provocative to say the least, for the Al Khalifa claimed that

Zubara belonged to them. When they heard that the village was being rebuilt and that a Turkish representative was preparing to hoist the Ottoman flag over the new settlement, they became extremely agitated. The British ambassador in Constantinople made an official protest, and H.M.S. *Sphinx* sailed for Zubara to demand the immediate return of the Al bin Ali. When Sheikh Sultan refused, the *Sphinx* seized some of his boats, causing him to change his mind. Now he wished to be reconciled with the Ruler of Bahrain. But by this time the Turks and Jasim had seen their chance. The Al bin Ali were prevented from returning to Bahrain, and while the Turkish governor in Hasa assembled a force on the mainland, Jasim collected a fleet of boats on the coast near Zubara. Their intentions seemed plain enough.

Realizing the situation was becoming critical, the British called in two more warships, the *Pigeon* and the *Plassey*, to help the *Sphinx* to patrol the sea between Bahrain and Qatar. At one point they even requested a battalion of infantry from Bombay, but the order was cancelled. Simultaneously, further warnings were issued to the Turks from London and in Constantinople.

None of these measures seemed to have the slightest effect. It was now high summer, and all day long the British warships cruised up and down the Qatar coast in sweltering heat, waiting for the enemy to move. On 19 August the Turkish governor of Hasa wrote a threatening letter to the British Resident warning him that he was no longer able to hold back Jasim's fleet, and advising that all British subjects should be evacuated from Bahrain within seventeen days. For a while the stalemate continued. Then, on 5 September, news reached Bahrain that the Turks had boarded H.M.S. *Pigeon* and demanded her immediate departure. Commander Pelly, the senior British naval officer, sailed at once for Zubara. There he found Jasim's fleet armed and ready to put to sea. The Turkish ultimatum of 19 August had by now expired and Pelly decided that the only way of saving Bahrain from invasion was to attack. He gave one hour's notice, and when this produced no answer, the *Sphinx* and the *Pigeon* went into action and quickly destroyed the Arab fleet. The next morning the Turks had disappeared from the scene and Jasim sued for peace, claiming unconvincingly that the invading force had only been assembled on the orders of the Turks.

Most of the Al bin Ali, with the exception of their leader, Sultan bin Salamah, returned to Bahrain together with over 100 boats captured by the British warships. A few months later, Jasim was informed that he would have to pay a fine of 30,000 rupees to recover this fleet. But he refused, and in April 1896 the boats were burnt at sea off the coast of Bahrain. Shortly afterwards a notice was pinned up in the Bahrain bazaars announcing that trade between the two states could be resumed. As in the past, the sudden squall had quickly blown over. From now on fears of an invasion of Bahrain from Qatar slowly died away.

By playing such a prominent part in this venture, Jasim had once again fallen foul of the British. He was always quick to repair such damage, however, and had a remarkable facility for behaving as though he had done nothing to cause offence. It was no surprise therefore to find him, only two years after the attempted invasion of Bahrain, renewing his request for an understanding with the British. The suggestion was made by Ahmed on Jasim's behalf when the political agent visited Wakrah on 25 November 1899 in connection with a piracy. Nothing was done at the time, but when the British set up an agency in Bahrain in 1900, Ahmed continued to

make overtures. In return for a promise of protection, he claimed, the Al Thanis were willing to settle on any part of the Qatar coast and be responsible for maintaining law and order in the district.

It is curious that the British did not take up his offer. They seemed to feel that it was not quite the moment for such a move. There were several reasons for their attitude. To start with, the Qatar coast had been remarkably free of trouble for many years, with the exception of 1899, when Bani Hajir pirates plundered a number of cargo boats. There was also a dramatic encounter off the coast of Wakrah in 1900 between the Amamara tribe and the Al bin Ali – the same people whose emigration from Bahrain had caused the crisis five years earlier. A blood-feud had existed between these two tribes ever since Sultan bin Salamah, the Al bin Ali chief, was shot dead by some Amamara while he was alone in his boat. Later some of the Al bin Ali had moved to Wakrah. One day in the summer of 1900 when they were pearl diving a few miles off the Qatar coast, five Amamara boats were suddenly blown into their midst by an adverse wind. Unable to believe their luck, the Al bin Ali gave the customary signal of battle by raising their flags. The Amamara replied with a fusillade of shots, but further action was prevented by the intervention of a nephew of Sheikh Jasim and the hapless intruders were allowed to leave without their arms. When the British Resident came to investigate the matter, he found the Al bin Ali to blame and fined them 1,000 rupees.

This had been one of the few incidents around the Qatar coast, and the British may have thought that it was no longer so important to come to terms with the Al Thani sheikhs. The other reason why Ahmed's overtures were in the end ignored was that the British government in

London did not for the moment want to alter the balance of power in Qatar. It continued to deny that the Turks had any rights in the peninsula, and when it was reported in 1902 that Turkish agents were to be stationed at Zubara, Odeid and Wakrah, the British protested vigorously. Attempts were made to prevent the officials from reaching their destinations. The agent for Wakrah did manage to take up his post, but he was soon withdrawn, and when one of Jasim's sons was appointed in his place, a fresh protest secured his dismissal too. These Turkish schemes were opposed in London because they would have upset the status quo in the peninsula; and it was for the same reason that any British agreement with the Al Thani sheikhs was also rejected. Another fourteen years were to pass before Qatar finally joined the trucial system.

Meanwhile the Turks clung to their precarious

foothold in Doha. The garrison, about 200 strong, was often weakened by desertions, but it enabled Turkey to keep control of Qatar's foreign policy. In domestic matters, however, the Turks were more like subjects than rulers. Hermann Burchardt, who in 1904 became the first European to cross the interior of the peninsula, reported that the Bedouin levied taxes on Turkish officers. And when he asked for permission to take photographs in Doha, he was referred by the Turkish commandant to the Al Thanis. At night-time the garrison lived in a state of apprehension. Sentries were posted at several places because the Arabs were well-armed, not only with Martinis, but also with magazine rifles.

Jasim was now an old man, well over eighty. He lived in retirement in Luseil, a village fifteen miles north of Doha, and left the administration of day-to-day affairs in the hands of his brother Ahmed. When Captain Prideaux, the Political Agent in Bahrain, visited Luseil in November 1905, he found the old sheikh as alert and healthy as ever. He was still keenly interested in political affairs, and it soon became apparent to Prideaux that nothing of any importance took place in Qatar without his being consulted. Ahmed was jealous of Jasim's lingering power, and on more than one occasion the two brothers failed to see eye to eye.

The friction between the brothers was abruptly ended when Ahmed was murdered by one of his own servants, a Bani Hajir who bore him a grudge. Jasim handled the emergency with his usual skill. Summoning the Bani Hajir tribe to his camp, he made them promise that they would hunt down and execute the murderer. During the meeting one of the Bani Hajir sheikhs was suddenly attacked and killed by a slave of Ahmed's. It looked as though the Al Thanis had taken their own summary revenge. But Jasim managed to soothe the tribesmen, and shortly afterwards Ahmed's murderer was caught and shot and the threat of a blood-feud between the parties passed away.

Jasim's rule was now drawing to a close. For over forty years he had been the most powerful sheikh in Qatar. From a precarious base he had slowly expanded his influence over the whole peninsula until, even in his last years, when he retired to Luseil, he alone had the authority to control the local tribesmen. He had seen off the Sheikh of Bahrain, except from his enclave in Zubara; he had handled the British with a mixture of effrontery and cunning; and towards the Turks he had maintained an attitude of insolent indifference which had come close to making their position in Qatar untenable. He did not live quite long enough to witness their final departure, for on 17 July 1913 he died, and was buried at Luseil. He was succeeded by his son Abdulla, who was, like his father, to rule for a long period, during which he would complete much of the work that Jasim had begun.

In 1913 life in Qatar had changed very little since Palgrave's visit exactly fifty years before. W. G. Lorimer, the colonial civil servant who wrote an exhaustive history of the Gulf, estimated the settled population of the country at around 27,000 at the turn of the century, excluding nomadic Bedouin tribesmen. The great majority of the people lived in Doha and Wakrah, while the rest were scattered in little villages such as Ruwais and Fuwairet on the north and east coasts of the peninsula. Like Palgrave, Lorimer was unimpressed by Doha:

'The general appearance of Doha is unattractive. The lanes are narrow and irregular, the houses dingy and small. There are no date palms or other trees, and the only garden is a small one near the fort, kept up by the Turkish garrison.'

Pearl diving was still almost the sole occupation of the people, and by now Qatar had 800 boats with 13,000 men working on the banks – the second largest fleet in the Gulf after Bahrain. A less important but profitable activity was the arms trade. In the last decade of the nineteenth century the Gulf had become a market place for arms, serving the people of Persia, Turkish Iraq, Central Arabia and even the tribesmen of Afghanistan and the North-West Frontier of India. The great majority of the weapons were British, and they were imported into the Gulf almost entirely through Muscat. Around the turn of the century the British succeeded in persuading the rulers of Bahrain and the Trucial States to ban the arms trade, and thereafter it slowly declined. But in Turkish-occupied Qatar there was no such prohibition, and Doha became a distribution point for arms destined for Persia and Central Arabia. By 1906 as many as 2,000 rifles a month were arriving in the town by sailing boat from Muscat. This reflected Qatar's continuing isolation from the rest of the Gulf.

Excluded from the trucial system, the country remained a law unto itself.

But not for long. Events on the international scene, and closer to home, were about to take a hand in Qatar's future. In Europe the big powers were on the brink of war. In the Gulf, British supremacy was being challenged for the first time for centuries: the French were entrenched in Muscat; the Germans had started a steamer service linking the Gulf with the Mediterranean; and the Germans and the Russians had plans to construct railways through Turkey and Persia respectively. And as the European powers competed with each other, the Turks slowly but inexorably weakened. The Wahabis had already recovered their ancestral possessions in Central Arabia from the Rashids, and in the spring of 1913 they turned their attention to the Turks and drove them out of Hasa. Ibn Saud, the Wahabi Amir, allowed them to keep their troops in the province, but from then on the Turkish garrison in Qatar was beleaguered. The Turks had already renounced all their claims to the peninsula in a separate treaty signed with the British, and arrangements had been made for them to withdraw from Doha. But the agreement was never ratified and the garrison was still there when war broke out between the two countries on 31 October 1914. Almost a year passed before the Turks finally took their leave. Sir Percy Cox, the British Resident in the Gulf, described the circumstances of their evacuation in a dispatch to the Secretary to the Government of India, dated 28 August 1915:

'On 16th August Trevor suggested that his Majesty's ship, *Pyramus* which was about to proceed to Kuwait and Bahrain to search for Tangistani dhows should also proceed to Al Bida (Doha) for the same purpose accompanied by Political Agent Bahrain. I concurred and instructed Political Agent Bahrain at the same time to ascertain exact state of affairs as regards Turkish garrison and guns and if possible to induce Shaikh for a consideration to get rid of Turks and hand over guns. Report from Political Agent Bahrain now received. Shaikh was amenable. The remainder of the Turkish garrison consisting of two officers and forty men disappeared during the night following interview with Shaikh, and with co-operation of latter a party from *Pyramus* with Political Agent Bahrain landed next morning and explored Fort. Breech blocks and cordite charges of the two field guns and one mountain gun had been removed but the guns and 500 projectiles were taken over by *Pyramus* and the Fort handed over to the Shaikh. Therefore, as far as Turkish garrison is concerned Katar question is disposed of.'

The departure of the Turks from Qatar after forty-four years opened the way for the British to negotiate the treaty which they had so often contemplated. Abdulla was friendly, but he was also on good terms with Ibn Saud, and for a time it was not at all certain which way he would jump. Shortly before the Turks had left, the Viceroy in India had written: 'The fact is that between Bin Saud and the Turks and ourselves, he does not know quite where he is.' Now the Turks had gone, but Saud looked correspondingly more powerful, and the British feared that he might suddenly annex Qatar and then turn on the other Trucial States. In the event, these fears proved unfounded. During December 1915 the Wahabi leader agreed to respect the independence of Qatar; and on 3 November of the following year, Sheikh Abdulla signed a treaty with the British. Qatar had at last become part of the trucial system.

From Penury to Prosperity

The British were delighted at their treaty with Qatar, and after the war in Europe was over they decided to reward Sheikh Abdulla for his friendship. The deputy Political Agent made a special trip to Doha for the occasion. After suitable speeches had been exchanged, Abdulla learnt that he had been given the companionship of the Most Eminent Order of the Indian Empire in recognition of his 'loyal and friendly conduct towards the British Government'. And as a further mark of esteem, he was to receive a personal salute of seven guns on all formal occasions.

Abdulla appears to have been well-pleased with these quaint imperial trophies. But if the British thought that they would be sufficient to buy his unstinting cooperation in the future, they were mistaken. The sheikh had already revealed himself as a tough negotiator with a shrewd grasp of how far he could go. He had wrung several concessions from Sir Percy Cox in the discussions which preceded the signing of the treaty. In a separate letter it had been agreed that, for the time being, no British subjects should be allowed to live in Qatar and that no British agent would be appointed to Doha without the sheikh's consent. This was a considerable triumph for Abdulla who, like his father before him, did not relish the prospect of foreigners sitting on his doorstep. It was not until after the Second World War that the British finally managed to install an agent in Doha.

Abdulla also succeeded in persuading his new allies to take an understanding view about the numerous slaves in his household, for Sir Percy Cox had written to him:

'And whereas you have represented to me that you and your dependants possess a good many slaves from of old time . . . accordingly I inform you that I recognise how you are placed in regard to this question and that supposing that you accord your negroes fair and just treatment, there will not be interference on the part of Government representatives in the matter.'

Sir Percy's accommodating attitude was probably influenced by the fact that most slaves were treated as family retainers.

Abdulla further demonstrated his ingenuity by capitalizing on what appears to have been an extraordinary misprint in a clause of the treaty that dealt with the sale of arms. Like the rulers of the other Trucial States, Abdulla was required to ban the arms trades in his territory, but as a gesture of goodwill, the British had made him a present of 300 rifles. In the text of the agreement, the phrase 'early delivery' of this consignment appeared as 'yearly'. Abdulla, naturally, took this literally, and was forever pressing the British to honour their commitment, though why he should need so many weapons and what was to become of them he never explained.

But on the whole the sheikh was very amenable, and conditions in and around the coast of Qatar improved dramatically compared with the anarchy which had prevailed during the Turkish occupation. After 1928 the Political Agent in Bahrain was made directly responsible for affairs in Qatar, and from time to time the various occupants of the post visited the peninsula to see that all was well. These excursions were often very exhausting experiences. The agent would travel to Qatar either by launch or occasionally by flying boat. Once he arrived in Doha, his problems really began. It was not unusual for him to find the Ruler away on one of his hunting expeditions in the interior, where he had to be tracked down sometimes fifty or sixty miles away. To avoid these pursuits, later agents in Bahrain always arranged their visits to Doha in advance. But there was nothing anybody could do about the heat. At the height of summer the temperature was invariably well over 100°F (38°C), and even the English colonial officer, with his love of the midday sun, tended to wilt. Describing a visit made one August to Qatar an agent wrote:

'It appears to be my fate to strike heat waves in Doha and the weather was exceptionally hot with a gharbi wind blowing and the Shaikh's country house at Rayan like a furnace. In fact I spent most of my spare time sitting in a well.'

It was not always that bad. Some agents seem to have positively enjoyed their trips to Qatar where they were completely free to punish the local miscreants in any way they saw fit. Captain R. G. Alban's visit to Doha in 1927 was typical. He arrived in H.M.S. *Lupin*, which had to anchor eight miles off the coast because of the local reefs. He had come to check that some men who had seized a former slave from a Bahrain boat were being punished. After establishing that the culprits had been put in prison, he presided over the burning of their boats in Doha harbour – with evident relish, to judge from his diary:

'The boat was accordingly drenched with kerosene oil and set alight. There were some 60 pearling boats in the harbour at the time and the blaze which was clearly visible from the Lupin eight miles off, provided them with an excellent object lesson; the whole town, of course, was also present at the spectacle.'

Yet such trivial incidents were soon forgotten in the disaster which was about to overtake Qatar, and indeed the whole Gulf. In the late 1920s the pearl trade suddenly fell into a slump from which it was never to recover. Pearling had always been a chancy business. A spell of bad weather, a poor crop of oysters, the mounting cost of provisioning the fleet – any one of these factors could make for a bad season with severe hardship resulting all along the coast. But these

were passing hazards, and a setback in one year was usually followed by recovery in the next. Now the trade was faced by a much greater and more permanent threat. The Japanese had invented the cultured pearl, and throughout the markets of the world this cheaper synthetic product was supplanting the original. To make matters worse, the rich countries of the West were in the grip of an economic recession, and each year fewer European and Indian dealers came to the Gulf to barter for the local pearls.

The effect on the Gulf states was catastrophic. In a few years prices fell by as much as 90 per cent, and the numbers of men working in the pearling fleets almost as drastically. Various belated attempts were made to protect the industry. Bahrain banned the import of modern diving equipment and outlawed the trade in cultured pearls. But these measures were no more than a gesture of defiance. In Qatar the situation was desperate. The British Agent in Bahrain reported in 1930: 'Qatar is worse hit than Bahrain by the depression . . . the customs dropped 50 per cent.' The next year he commented: 'The bulk of the inhabitants are on the verge of destitution . . . people have sold the rafters of their homes to maintain themselves.'

It was at this moment, as we saw at the outset, that the fortunes of the country changed. For some years it had been thought that oil might be found in the peninsula, and a geological survey carried out in 1932 confirmed these hopes. The next year negotiations for the concessions began. Sheikh Abdullah was as skilful as ever when it came to striking a bargain, and it was not until 1935, after a lot of haggling over details, that the oil concession was finally signed. Abdulla received a down-payment of £400,000 in return for surrendering exclusive rights over Qatar to the oil companies for seventy-five years. It was not much compared with the enormous revenues of the future, but in the depressed conditions of the time it must have been very welcome. True to form, the British presented Abdulla with another medal.

Over the next few years a small band of foreigners, supported by 300 local workers, set up a camp on the western side of the peninsula and began to drill for oil. For Abdulla and his people the success of the operation must have seemed the only possible hope for the future of their country. But no sooner had the good news of the oil strike been received, than the promised bonanza faded before their eyes. War had once again broken out in Europe. Before even a single drop of oil could be shipped from Qatar, the wells were first plugged and then later stripped and destroyed in case they should fall into the hands of the Germans. The oil companies informed Abdulla that they would have to cut down on the services they had supplied in the past: they would continue to send a weekly dhow from Bahrain to the camp at Dukhan with the mail; but instead of the car service they operated between the camp and Doha, there would now only be camels. And no more help could be given in repairing the Ruler's cars. More importantly, the local employees would be discharged with one month's pay. An oil com-

Souk trader, Doha

Coffee time

Fishmonger, Doha

Market Place,
Doha

Market Place, Doha

Repairing nets

pany operator described their departure from Dukhan cheerfully: 'It is reported that parties of labourers leaving the camp on termination have been in high spirits and seem very satisfied.'

Their optimism cannot have lasted long, however, for the situation in Qatar had by now reached a very low ebb. The British Agent in Bahrain remarked on 'the extreme poverty' of the people, many of whom were starving and only being kept alive by an irregular supply of food quotas provided by the British. Pearl diving continued fitfully, but the trade had not recovered. A lot of boats were broken up and used as firewood, while others were sailed away by their owners in search of a better life in India, East Africa or other parts of the Gulf. Some reports suggested that mass emigration had reduced the population to under 10,000 – less than half what it had been during the First World War.

This desperate state of affairs was made even worse by the suspension of all trade with Bahrain following a renewed outbreak of hostility between the two states over Zubara. Many years had passed since the last episode in this running conflict, and by the 1930s it seemed that the issue was dead. The town was almost deserted and it was widely assumed to have become part of Qatar by force of circumstance, if for no other reason. It was all the more unexpected, therefore, when Bahrain protested fiercely at Sheikh Abdulla's plans to build a customs post at Zubara.

The first round of the negotiations which followed were held in Bahrain and produced no agreement. The scene then moved to the village of Al Ghariyeh on the north-east coast of Qatar. The Bahrain delegation, consisting of several sheikhs and a retinue of followers, arrived in two launches, while Abdulla travelled up from Doha overland. The talks were held in a tent on the edge of the village, but after several days' discussion the two sides were still deadlocked and the Bahrainis returned home. Shortly after, a skirmish took place at Zubara between Abdulla's supporters and some Naim tribesmen. The Naim lost, and most of them then emigrated from Qatar. But the damage had been done, and for several years, at a most critical moment in their history, the two states had little to do with each other.

It was some time before conditions improved in Qatar after the war. Drilling only started again in the oil fields in 1947, and the first ship-load of oil did not leave until two years later. But, by then, the prosperity of the country was assured, and from all directions people flocked back to the homes they had only recently deserted. For the first time in thirty years there was enough work to go round. Sheikh Abdulla did not live quite long enough to see the new world which was about to come into existence. He survived Hamad, his younger son and chosen successor, by two years, and died in 1949. During the rule of his successors, Sheikh Ali and Sheikh Ahmed, Qatar began to change rapidly as the oil revenue mounted.

But it was only when the present Ruler, Sheikh Khalifa, came to power that the country emerged from the backwater it had occupied for so long, and began to play a leading role in the affairs of the Gulf. Sheikh Khalifa had already presided over the final act of the political emancipation of the state. On 1 September 1971 the treaty with Britain was ended, and, having decided against joining the United Arab Emirates, Qatar, like Bahrain, became an independent power. The ambitions of Sheikh Khalifa's great-grandfather Jasim, who more than anyone could claim to be the founder of the country, had at last been realized.

Photography by Aerofilms Ltd.

Aerial view of Doha

Aerial view of Doha

Photography by Aerofilms Ltd.

Aerial view of Doha

Part Two

Qatar Today

The City of Doha

The road from Doha to Saudi Arabia travels south-west for sixty miles, more or less following the path of the old pilgrim route to Mecca. Until a few years ago it was no more than a rough track, almost indistinguishable from the surrounding flat, stony desert. It was nevertheless well worn, for this was the only clearly marked link between Qatar and the Arabian hinterland. Except for the Bedouin, who have always ranged freely through the desert, almost every overland traveller between the peninsula and Central Arabia came this way. It was the route chosen by the explorer Hermann Burchardt when he visited Doha in 1904. And thirty years later Sheikh Abdulla had travelled along the same path in the opposite direction when he went to see Ibn Saud in Riyadh. Then camels were the sole means of transport, and the journey lasted several days, with five staging posts at wells along the way – the only landmarks on the open desert plain.

The scenery has hardly changed today, but the journey is very different. At the border post at Selwa heavily laden lorries sit with their engines idling as they pause before completing the last lap in a journey which may have begun more than 3,000 miles away in Europe. Then sometimes alone, sometimes in convoys of two or three, they set out on a wide, tarmac'd highway which has been carved out of the desert. For a few miles the road winds through the low, wind-eroded ridges of the western coast. Thereafter the land is flat and the lorries pound along across a plain where only the silhouette of a solitary camel or a clump of date trees breaks the horizon. After twenty-five miles they pass through Karana, one of the staging posts on the old pilgrim route and now a dusty village dominated by an elegant hunting lodge belonging to a former ruler of Qatar; in the 1950s, the main entrance of the lodge had to be widened to allow a roast camel to pass through for a banquet being held in honour of a visiting sheikh. A few miles further on the lorries come to Mukeinis, another staging post for travellers in the past and now the site of an earth satellite station, a startling anomaly in this primitive landscape. Then the road straightens out for the final run into Doha. Sometimes in the early morning or late afternoon you will see a car pulled up by the roadside and the driver, on his knees beside it, bowing down towards Mecca. But otherwise little distracts the eye until, less than an hour after leaving the border, the outline of the capital shows up ahead.

Doha is the symbol of modern Qatar, a magnet which draws everything and everyone towards it. Since the Second World War the country's population has increased from 25,000 to more than 200,000, and at least 80 per cent now live in or around the capital. Immigrants outnumber the local people, and more arrive each year because Qatar, like many other Gulf states, is short of manpower, especially skilled workers. In some parts of the town the green and white Pakistani flag is seen as often as the white and purple colours of Qatar.

Doha is the country's warehouse. Almost every object has to be imported to feed the maelstrom of development unleashed by oil. The daily procession of lorries coming from Saudi Arabia is only one part of a continuous sea, land and air operation. Every day of the week, jet aeroplanes fly in across the bay with their latest consignment of businessmen and tech-

nicians, while the raw materials arrive by sea. In the past ships sometimes had to queue up for ninety days before they could unload their cargoes on the harbour's quays where they join an ever-expanding mountain of goods waiting to be collected. The delay is now much shorter since the capacity of the harbour has been increased.

Someone who has never been to Doha before realizes immediately that he has arrived in a frontier town. His first impression is of one vast construction site echoing day and night to the rumble of concrete mixers. In the evening light the silhouettes of cranes compete with minarets against the city skyline, and work often goes on all night in a never-ending cycle of demolition and reconstruction. Doha already has its landmarks: the Grand Mosque with its slim minaret and, near by, the Emiri Palace built on a slight rise of the ground overlooking the harbour.

These elegant achievements give some idea of what the city may look like in five or ten years' time. For the moment it is still taking shape, and everywhere there are new buildings at various stages of development and in a giddy variety of architectural styles: shining glass and concrete monoliths on the seafront, government ministries in the more subdued Arabic style and acres of simple box-like houses in the suburbs. The fever of construction is so great that all around the perimeter of the town the desert has been marked off with breezeblocks, sometimes only two bricks high, by individuals eager to stake their claim in time for the next wave of expansion. As one visitor remarked, there is enough building going on in Doha to support the concrete industry of the whole world.

This frenzied activity gives the town an uninhibited atmosphere of vitality. It is as though someone had decreed that Doha should be built, if not in a day, then in a year; and in pursuit of this goal everyone is naturally in a hurry. There are few rules or restrictions to observe. Driving habits are haphazard, and many of the expensive new cars which race around the wide boulevards still have their sales tickets sticking to their windows. Sometimes the street lighting blazes away all day, reminding anyone who happens to notice that here, at least, money is no problem.

In these surroundings it is almost impossible to remember that, not so long ago, Doha was a little fishing and pearling village unknown to the outside world. Even as late as the 1950s the most

ordinary modern amenities had not yet arrived. Water was still brought in by tanker from outside the town and rationed at ten gallons a head. Electricity was provided for a few people by generators. There was no drainage of any kind, and when it rained very heavily the water would pour down to the sea from the desert, forming a channel through the town large enough for boats to sail on. Air conditioning was unheard of: in the *souk* the merchants used to gain relief from the oppresive heat by raising a cloth on a pole through the roof to catch the passing breeze. Communications with the outside world were sporadic. The weekly plane which brought the mail often did not bother to land; it would circle around two or three times and then drop its load by parachute. In the harbour there were only two small jetties. One belonged to the Ruler while the other was always crowded with camels, skins, fish and other local merchandise.

This simple life has long since disappeared, but here and there a few relics remain hemmed in by the growing modern city. There is still a camel market in Doha. One last wind-tower survives as a monument to the age before air conditioning. The *souk* has not yet been rebuilt. And on the corniche which rolls around Doha bay you often see fishermen mending their nets on the pavement as the Cadillac and Mercedes cars speed past a few yards away.

But the most conspicuous reminder of the

past is the National Museum on the seafront. Seventy years ago this building was the home of Sheikh Abdulla, who chose the spot so that he could remain at some distance from the Turkish headquarters in the centre of the town. Soon after the Turks left, Abdulla moved out, leaving the place to his sons Ali and Hamad, and it was here that the present Ruler, Sheikh Khalifa, spent much of his childhood. After the war the palace was abandoned and gradually fell into ruins. But, a few years later, Sheikh Khalifa, realizing that modern development would soon completely obliterate the past, decided to restore the buildings and turn them into a museum.

The result is a most striking symbol of modern Doha. For the museum compound, with its network of white-washed buildings restored exactly in the old Arabic architectural style, and its cool, well-watered lawns and shrubs, stands in the middle of several acres of flattened rubble: an oasis of preservation in a desert of development. Inside, various aspects of the seafaring and Bedouin society of the past are displayed in a manner as graceful as that of any museum in the world. The compound includes a lagoon with samples of several Arab dhows now seldom seen in the Gulf: bateels, bagharas, booms and sambuks. And, near by, meticulously preserved, sit the stately Cadillacs which once belonged to Sheikh Khalifa's father and grandfather. The back seats of these heavy black vehicles consisted of two armchairs which swung forward to eject their occupants at the touch of a button. Even these comparatively modern machines seem to conjure up a vanished world in the Doha of the 1970s.

Yet, for all Sheikh Khalifa's attempts to preserve the past, it is inevitably the present, and even more the future, which preoccupies people in Doha; and so the Museum of Modern Development half a mile away from the old Al Thani palace is a more accurate reflection of the town. Built in the same traditional style, it stands across the square from the Emiri Palace, and here you can see in a series of lighted diagrams and illustrations how the vast oil revenues are being spent. The transformation of the country during the last twenty-five years, and especially in the last five since Sheikh Khalifa took over the government, is astonishing. (It is not so much the process of modernization in Qatar which is exceptional, since many other countries are undergoing the same experience; it is the speed at which it is happening.)

Where there was one school with 250 pupils in 1952, there are now 108 with more than 31,000 schoolchildren. The solitary hospital with a single resident doctor of 1945 has been turned into four medical centres and 100 specialists, with another 600-bedroom hospital nearly finished. The large ships which in the past had to anchor eight miles off Doha now berth at the deep-water port a few hundred yards out in the bay. And standing several miles outside the town in the desert, like some colossal protuberance, there is the 40,000-capacity stadium where the 1976 Fourth Arabian Gulf Football Tournament was held.

All these projects have already been completed. For an idea of what will soon follow, one has only to walk across the square to the Emiri Palace where the Ruler's advisers on town planning have their offices. Like most planners, they are highly articulate visionaries, and with frequent references to drawings and beautifully constructed models, they outline the future city already taking shape outside their windows. Its success, they claim, will depend on a synthesis of past and present.

One planner believes that 'the old architecture is not suited to such things as cars and air-conditioning which are here to stay whatever one may think of them'. The vocabulary of that style was not enough. It must be used, but has to be adapted to modern needs.

The point is illustrated by several projects still on the drawing board. One is a futuristic-looking pyramidic hotel which will be built on reclaimed land at the far end of the bay. Another is a sixty-foot arabesque tower rising from the sea in the centre of the harbour. Both are projects which combine traditional Arab architecture with modern technology.

Other schemes include a new airport, to be built ten miles west of Doha (the present one is already being engulfed by the rapid expansion of the town); the redevelopment of the *souk*, with a warren of courtyards and air-conditioned corridors; and the construction of a university. This project is in many ways the most interesting. One feature of the design is an attempt to apply the principle of the wind-tower to the students' quarters. The dome-shaped roofs will have four openings in each direction, and tests in wind tunnels have shown that they can catch the air and channel it into the rooms below. Most modern buildings in Doha are totally unequipped to deal with the heat when the air-conditioning breaks down; should this happen in the future, the students will be sitting coolly on their campus while the merchants in down-town Doha steam in their modern office blocks.

These grandiose schemes, of course, are the stuff that planners' dreams are made of, and to realize them is not quite as easy as the original neat little models suggest. One overwhelming problem facing anyone trying to create an ordered city in Qatar is the fierce independence of the people. It is all very well laying down standards of building and design in land being developed by the government; to try to impose the same standards on individuals is another matter. Thus compulsory purchase is a rare

event in Qatar. During the last few years, land values have followed the predictable spiralling pattern of a boom town. In the *souk* a square foot of land can fetch up to £150, and even in the desert outside Doha it seldom costs less than £10. As prices rise, people become increasingly reluctant to sell, so the government finds it cheaper to reclaim land from the sea than purchase it in the open market. No wonder people hurry to reserve their allotments. This free-for-all would be tolerated in few other places, but here the rights of the individual are respected on even the most tenuous grounds. Someone may claim that he has always grazed his sheep on a particular plot of desert, or landed his fishing boat at a certain spot on the coastline, and that will often be enough to establish his ownership.

For the same reason, a man can build what he likes on his own land, and in Doha that can mean almost anything. The desert people's love for bright colours, so forcibly illustrated on most forms of local transport and in the strange proliferation of tartan suitcases, is really indulged when it comes to decorating a home. The windows and doors of even the most modern houses are often picked out in a bold design of red, orange or yellow paint.

But the showpieces of Doha are the fantastic villa-palaces which have risen up along the roads leading out of the town in the last few years. Each building is set back in a compound surrounded by high walls extending for up to a hundred yards and painted in a wide range of exotic colours. The centrepiece of each extravaganza is usually a triumphant archway, elaborately carved and decorated. At one palace north of Doha yellow walls have been matched with magenta arches, but they are no more discordant than many others. Most of these palaces stand alone in the desert, and against their austere background they look like fairy castles borrowed from a theatrical set. But they are very much part of the scenery of modern Doha, and like the breezeblocks outside the town they will probably continue to foil the planners' ordered designs.

Old mosque, Old Wakrah

The Pearl Trade

For the older generation of Qataris the transformation of Doha from fishing village to modern city has been a bewildering experience. It is scarcely possible to exaggerate the extremes of poverty and wealth that a man now in his sixties will have witnessed. He will remember, for instance, the kind of depressing conditions described by the British Political Agent in Bahrain on 14 March 1934:

'There has been no rain in Qatar, and the spring grazing has failed. Economic conditions are very bad. A recently returned doctor reports that poverty is very marked . . . many people do not have enough to eat.'

Today, only forty years later, the same man could read in a survey made by the World Bank that Qatar is one of the three richest countries in the world in terms of per capita income.

One might have thought that so great a reversal of fortune would have created a boundless faith in the future. But the local people remain oddly sceptical, as though they did not quite believe what has happened, or at any rate expected the bonanza to vanish as quickly as it had appeared. For the time being all is well, they will say, and beyond that they will not go.

What they cannot deny is that the Qatari of the 1970s is a different man from his predecessors. He is not simply richer: his whole way of life has changed. 'I have led two lives – before and after oil,' remarks a local painter, and that is true of almost everyone. In a matter of a few years oil has propelled the country out of a simple village economy into an industrialized society. In the process some occupations have completely disappeared, some have been revitalized and some, previously unheard of in Qatar, have been imported from abroad.

If one searches out the modern Qatari one no longer finds him only on a dhow or camped in a tent in the desert. Nowadays he is more likely to be in a merchant's office, a factory or a government ministry. Yesterday's pearl divers have become today's teachers, civil servants and industrial technicians.

Pearl diving, which was to the past what oil-drilling has been to the present, has been one of the casualties of the new prosperity. In the whole of Qatar there is not one active professional diver left. The discovery of oil did not immediately kill the industry. Even after the war people continued to dive, simply because there was nothing else for them to do. One Englishman, who has lived in Qatar for the last twenty-five years, remembers that there were still two boats going out when he arrived. For the first six months he lived in a house which had been the pearl court, where shares of the catch were determined for each member of a boat's crew. The building, like many others, has long since disappeared and is now the site of the Qatar National Bank.

It was only when the oil began to flow that the last divers gave up. The better working conditions and pay offered by the oil companies proved irresistible, and from all over the coast people converged on the oil fields of Dukhan. But they did not easily forget the pearl banks as the Shell Oil Company discovered when it began its off-shore operations in the early 1950s. When they first arrived, the company employed divers using modern machinery to install the oil rigs. Although pearling had virtually ceased by then, there was uproar among the local people who feared that the new equipment would enable the divers to strip the oyster beds clean. In the event they were reassured, but the taboo remains, and even today it is doubtful if anyone would be allowed to exploit the pearl beds by modern methods.

The pearls themselves have not disappeared from the Gulf. There may be no divers left, but a

few traders have carried on. In fact, according to one European dealer, Qatar has now become the leading centre for the pearl trade in the Gulf. This development has come about through one of those ironic twists of history which are totally unpredictable. Fifty years ago the main export route for pearls was either via India to Paris and London, or directly to the European capitals. As the depression set in, European dealers stopped coming to the Gulf and the trade was restricted to India where the pearls were refined and polished before being sent on to other parts of the world. So important was this outlet that when India temporarily banned the import of precious stones in 1947 to save foreign currency, panic seized the Gulf states. The ban was lifted, but the diving ceased shortly after.

Now, twenty-five years later, the market patterns of the past have been neatly reversed. Instead of exporting pearls, Qatar imports them. The local people, with a lot of money to spend, have discovered a taste for the jewels which once they could not afford to keep. Sheikh Khalifa is said to have a very good collection, and some of the finest specimens can be found among the merchant community in Doha. The pearls are imported from other Arab states, and even from Europe. One dealer recently claimed to have returned from a shopping expedition to Kuwait where he spent over a million pounds on pearls for the domestic market. The irony is, of course, that many of them must have originally come from the pearl banks around the coast of Qatar; and having passed from hand to hand through the capitals of the world over several decades, they are now returning to their source.

One need go no further than the *souk* in Doha for evidence of this process. Tucked away in the labyrinthine network of arcaded stalls there are several goldsmiths' and jewellers' shops. One of

them belongs to Muhammad Gawad Ali Gamal, a seventy-five-year-old man with a lean angular face and rimless glasses. Muhammad is the archetypal Qatari. Both his grandfather and father were pearl merchants, and he has himself been in the business for nearly sixty years.

'We were traders rather than divers,' he says, 'and our excursions on the sea were limited to those times when we sailed out in a small boat to the fleet to collect the pearls. At first we did well enough. But then, about forty years ago, things began to go badly. Trade declined and it affected everyone. I can remember a year when we made no money at all. But in those days there was nothing else to do. Pearls were our livelihood. There was no alternative.

'Later, after the oil came and nobody dived any more, I began dealing in gold jewellery. This was very profitable and I have continued with it ever since. But recently I started selling pearls again, and nowadays my turnover from them is far greater than it used to be even before the slump. People seem to want to buy them again, but now I have to get them from abroad.'

And to illustrate his point, Muhammad produced a double string of pearls from one of his showcases which he estimates to be worth £7,000. 'At that price I will have no difficulty in finding a customer,' he says.

In the circumstances, it is surprising that pearl diving has not been revived in Qatar, at least on a small scale. One might have expected some enterprising individual to capitalize on the presence of so many old pearling skills, and equip a fleet of boats. That it has not happened reflects the degree of prosperity oil has brought to the country. With so many easier and more rewarding ways of making a living, there is little incentive to return to the arduous and unhealthy business of diving. Occasionally one of the older men will take out a boat and spend the afternoon on a near-by pearl bank. But he dives merely for his own satisfaction, like someone who cannot forget an old habit; and nowadays the pearl banks from Bahrain to Dubai, once crowded for six months of the year with hundreds of boats, are deserted. So far as anyone knows, the oysters are still there.

The Merchants

Of all the various groups in Qatar, none has benefited more from the discovery of oil than the big merchant families. The Arabs of the Gulf have been trading for centuries, but never before have their potential rewards been so great. In Qatar, the commercial opportunities are particularly favourable: taxation is virtually non-existent and the need to import everything from a hammer to a new steel-plant leaves the field wide open for the clever entrepreneur. Those who have seized the chance have become the financial aristocracy of the new society. Starting as small-time traders dealing in coffee and dates, they are now multi-millionaire operators specializing in every kind of commercial activity from heavy industrial contracting to property development. In the suburbs of Doha they live in ornate villas that are often decorated in a confusion of the latest Western styles; and in the city centre they work in sleek, air-conditioned offices furnished in standard opulent businessmen's taste: comfortable sofas, fitted carpets, low perspex tables with at least one heavy expensive ashtray.

Here, all day long, a procession of British, Japanese and other businessmen troop in to present their wares. Deals are negotiated over interminable cups of tea and coffee, usually served by Indians, and then, once the mandatory visiting cards have been exchanged, the businessman is shown out to make way for another who is more often than not a direct competitor. Later in the evening the harassed foreigners can be seen eating a solitary meal at the Gulf Hotel, each seated at a separate table contemplating the day's struggle. In the Gulf it is a buyer's market these days and hard work for the visiting businessman.

Of all the big merchant families in Qatar, only two were of any importance before the present economic boom. One was the Darwish family,

the other the Al Mana. Between them they held such power that their fortunes were once almost synonymous with those of the whole country. Both families were traders and pearl merchants, and both made their money by becoming contractors to the oil companies, a relationship which has been the foundation of many a merchant's fortune in the Gulf.

The Al Mana family rose to prominence in the late 1920s when Saleh al Mana became the Ruler's secretary. Sheikh Abdulla was already getting old by then, and liked to spend his time hunting, and so much of the not very arduous day-to-day administration was left to his secretary. Saleh al Mana was a shrewd and efficient courtier whose family had attained a position in Qatar second only to the Al Thanis, the leading family in Qatar. It was they who received Bertram Thomas when he arrived in Doha at the end of his historic crossing of the Empty Quarter in 1931. The occasion is recorded in Thomas's account of his travels in a photograph which shows the leading members of the family posing solemnly with Sheikh Abdulla. (Thomas's subsequent arrival in Bahrain received only a passing mention from the British Agent. Under 'News about Foreigners' appeared the following item: 'Mr B. Thomas OBE, Financial Adviser to the Sultan of Muscat, arrived in Bahrain 20 February from Dhuzaf via Qatar.'

Saleh al Mana continued to be Abdulla's right-hand man through the 1930s and 1940s, and his goodwill was essential for anyone seeking favours from the Ruler. Successive British Agents in Bahrain cultivated it assiduously. When the Second World War broke out, Saleh was the only man in Qatar with a radio and people used to resort to his house in the evening to listen to the news. The radio must have eventually broken down for a few years later the British Agent sent him another set.

For one reason or another this radio and the replacement which followed it failed to work. Saleh returned the second one with a note asking for a different make. 'I believe,' he wrote, 'that this kind of set does not suit the Qatar climate.'

That was in 1947, and by then the position of the Al Manas was being challenged by the Darwish family. The Darwishes went into business when three brothers established a firm in 1911. They were pearl merchants, and also traded in foodstuffs, kerosene and other commodities. By the time the Second World War broke out, they had already become prominent in Doha. One of the brothers was Director of Customs, and the family business acted as agents for the Qatar Petroleum Company, as it was then called.

In the years after the war the family continued to consolidate its position. While Sheikh Abdulla relied on Saleh al Mana, his son Sheikh Hamad was very close to Abdulla Darwish, who, among other things, acted as his business manager; a report in the diaries of the Bahrain Agency notes how Darwish had arrived in Bahrain in 1946 to sell large quantities of pearls belonging to Sheikh Hamad. The alliance with Sheikh Hamad, together with their position as labour contractors to the returning oil company, cemented the family fortunes, and by the early 1950s the Darwishes were involved in practically every enterprise in Qatar.

A 1953 report on Doha prepared by a representative of Shell, then laying the foundations for its off-shore drilling operations, gives a glimpse of the variety of their interests. Remarking on the absence of suitable accommodation, the report says: 'As an initial measure a building has been rented from Abdulla Darwish . . . rent is Rs 2,000 per month for the block.' Later, referring to the need for more housing, it goes on: '. . . it is proposed to build permanent houses of concrete blocks (locally made) using the local

Footsteps in the sand

Sand dunes   Sand and sea

Bedouin

Goats

White oryx

Burning off

Irrigation

Tomato plants

Fruits of the desert

Shepherd with flock

Tomato plants

contractor Abdulla Darwish.' A typical house was to be designed by 'Darwish's engineer'.

These were indeed the Darwish years, and in 1953 Abdulla accompanied Sheikh.Ali's son to attend the coronation of Queen Elizabeth in London. From then on the family's power slowly declined. Abdulla Darwish fell out of favour and went to live on the Saudi Arabian coast. Later the family business was split into three parts. But even had this not happened, the monopoly enjoyed by the firm could hardly have survived. The vast projects under way in Qatar today are too big for one enterprise to handle, and inevitably competitors have moved in to exploit the opportunities. Names like the Mannai and Jaidah trading companies are now as conspicuous as those of the Al Manas and Darwishes.

Yet the two families remain the sole commercial link with the years of austerity before 1939. While Saleh al Mana and Abdulla Darwish spent most of their time in Doha or accompanying the sheikhs on hunting expeditions in the desert, their successors do business in the capitals of Western Europe. The scale of their operations is enormous. The Al Manas hold the concession for Peugeot, the best-selling car in Qatar; and down on the jetties of the harbour almost every lorry seems to bear the family imprint. The tentacles of the Darwish empire appear to embrace as much as ever – a recent advertisement for one branch of the business included the memorable claim: 'A very wide experience in civil contracting from schools to palaces'. Youssuf Darwish, whose offices near the Emiri Palace are pleasantly free from the ostentation of many others, does not regret the changes oil has brought. 'It may have been a simpler life with no social problems before,' he reflects, 'but today we have opportunities which were never even dreamed of then.'

Perhaps only a few can afford to dream on the scale of an Al Mana or a Darwish, but today even the least ambitious Qatari can become a successful businessman without having to work too hard. Doha has many smart shops managed by foreigners and owned by Qataris. They sell mostly luxury goods like watches and backgammon boards with Western brand-names, but occasionally a local symbol is borrowed to embellish some cosmopolitan product. 'Oryx pools', announces one sign: 'Swimming pools of distinction'.

The *souk* alone retains something of the intimate atmosphere which must have characterized the whole town, and here one can find those Qataris who have gravitated from the pearl banks to the market place. Muhammad Zeini, a small, serious man in his late sixties, is one of them.

'I used to own a boat in partnership with my brothers,' he says. 'In the summer we went pearling and for the rest of the year we sailed round the Gulf, carrying passengers and trading in dates, grain and flour. In a good season we used to make between 20,000 and 30,000 rupees. But it was a hard life and I left it as soon as I could. I was twenty-eight at the time, and I had already spent nearly sixteen years of my life at sea.'

As it did for everyone else, Muhammad's chance came with oil, but unlike many of his contemporaries he did not join the rush to the oil fields. He had always had some artistic ability, and had spent his spare time wood-carving and painting his home. He also embroidered clothes with gold threads in patterns based on his own designs. When the moment came he turned this hobby into a one-man cottage industry, working at first mainly for friends. This eventually led him to try his hand as a carpet dealer.

'I had to sell my house to raise the capital to buy the carpets,' he says, 'but there was money about for the first time. My business did well, and I was soon importing from Kuwait and even Europe, choosing designs which I thought would appeal to Qataris. Nowadays I make a lot more money than I ever did from pearl diving.'

Is he a happier man? Muhammad sat for a long while among his piles of carpets, watched by the usual throng of curious onlookers who invariably congregate in the *souk*, contemplating the question.

'It's a fine contrast,' he said eventually. 'In the past we were all physically exhausted but our hearts were calm. Now it is a tense life, and though we are better off, progress seems to bring difficulties.'

It is a refrain that one hears everywhere from the shop in the *souk* to the Bedouin tent in the desert.

The Civil Servants

One of the more striking innovations in modern Qatar is the ever-increasing role that the government plays in the lives of ordinary people and, correspondingly, the role that they play in the life of the government. Qataris are used to being left alone. Until quite recently the average man got on with his fishing or pearl diving and left everything else to the ruling Al Thani family. Sheikh Khalifa changed all that. During the past ten years he has transformed the government from a patriarchal, almost private affair into an instrument for running a modern state. The April 1970 provisional constitution confirmed the Al Thanis as hereditary rulers, and nearly all the important offices of state are held by members of the family. But nowadays there is also an advisory council made up of thirty leading citizens who have the power to summon ministers and question them about their policies.

It was Sheikh Khalifa's decision to distribute the oil revenues more equitably through the country which really drew people into the process of government. The state suddenly became the great provider. Education, medical care, transport, communications and a whole range of other services were laid on – many of them free. To man the ministries in charge of these colossal projects, an army of civil servants had to be recruited. In no time at all there were as many, if not more, bureaucrats in Doha as businessmen.

These men (nearly all working women are teachers) are well paid and usually installed in comfortable modern offices. They are not all local people. By law a minister has to be someone 'of Qatari origin' – which means anyone who lived in the country before 1930. Below him is a director who is sometimes an immigrant, but is nowadays more often a Qatari – one of the increasing number of graduates who have been educated abroad.

Many of these people are very hard working with demanding schedules to fulfil. But it sometimes seems as though there are too many of them with too little to do. Indeed, a recent government commission suggested that the civil service could be pruned by 10 per cent. That is certainly the impression one gets from visiting some departments, where the day seems to pass in pleasant coffee-shop conversation quite unlike the urgent bargaining which goes on in the local merchants' offices.

This is partly a difference in style: the bureaucrat inevitably lacks the businessman's aggressive competitiveness. But it also reflects the generosity of an affluent employer. With such abundant resources, the government can afford to look after everyone with perhaps a small measure of indulgence. If someone needs a job, then room can be found somewhere or other. To the outsider, this benevolence may seem only natural, a predictable extension of the deeply-ingrained Arab tradition of hospitality. The local people, for their part, seem to have accepted it with a mild sense of wonder. 'The government wants to help everyone,' explained one young Qatari with a mixture of admiration and incredulity.

A perfect example of this munificent attitude can be found in the occupation of an employee at the National Museum whose life personifies both Qatar's past and present. Sayid al Badid, like everyone else, grew up with pearls. He first went to sea with his father when he was only six, and four years later began working on the boats. For the next thirty years he made his living on the pearl banks, first as a diver and later as the captain of his own boat. Then came oil and Sayid bought a launch which he sailed up and down the Gulf, trading in dates and coffee. Ten years ago he retired from the sea and the government gave him a pension. But he

was not idle for long. When the National Museum opened in 1975, Sheikh Khalifa, who had known Sayid for many years, asked him to be the custodian of the dhows on the Museum's artificial lagoon.

And there he can now be found on any day of the week. Around him lie the beautifully preserved specimens of the very boats which once provided him with a more active way of life. It is a tranquil scene, disturbed only by the odd passing visitor. Sayid still owns his launch and occasionally hires it out to the Shell Oil Company. Sometimes he takes the boat himself and spends an afternoon diving for pearls which he gives away as presents. But otherwise he just sits guarding the lagoon, often in the shade on the deck of one of the dhows, passing the hours away with reminiscences about the past. Like the boats he looks after, he has become a museum piece.

The Students

At the other end of the spectrum from Sayid al Badid are the young generation of Qataris who are beginning to graduate from the new schools. In their spare time many of these students occupy themselves in ways which would not have been possible for their parents. One example is a group which assembles once a week in a colonnaded courtyard hidden behind a large door near the *souk*. On a particular evening last spring there were about twenty of them there, all under thirty. Most had come straight from work, and the only thing which distinguished them from people of their own age anywhere else in the world were the large cars in which they all arrived. The last to turn up were three girls who sat quietly on the sidelines and left the men to get things organized. There was not much to arrange: a green telephone, a table and a couple of chairs. When these were in place, everything was ready. One of Doha's theatre companies was about to begin rehearsals for its latest play.

Modern theatre has only just arrived in Qatar. Although there are three companies, all financially supported by the government, and plans exist to build a national theatre, it is still very much an amateur affair. The head of one group, for instance, is a health inspector by profession, and all the actors are part-time. Productions are staged at irregular intervals and for short periods. The record-breaking run of one recent play lasted fully fourteen nights.

It is remarkable, however, that a theatre exists at all, for the stage does not easily fit in with the strict rules of the Wahabi sect of Islam to which Qatar belongs. Objections to the setting up of a theatre came from all sides when the first group was formed in the 1960s. The suggestion that girls should appear on the stage was especially alarming. But slowly the opposition was broken down, and the theatre has come to be accepted along with other embryonic Qatar arts. Already it is turning into a forum where the young can express their ideas.

These are inevitably perplexing to older Qataris. Their children are the first generation to have grown up in an affluent world; they do not remember the hard times. An increasing number of them are sent to study abroad, and when they come home from Beirut, Cairo or London the combined experience of education and money makes them question the old established practices. Like their Western counterparts, they are more daring than their parents. They no longer want to live in the same house with them when they get married. The boys are passionate about football, and the girls believe they should be able to lead freer lives – all commonplace preoccupations in the West, but positively radical in Qatar. And along with this challenge to the old conventions, they criticize some of the values imported with the oil revenues.

The play being rehearsed in the courtyard that evening, one of three planned for performance on the anniversary of Sheikh Khalifa's succession, concerned a merchant who commissions a fourteen-storey block of flats. From the beginning everything goes wrong for him, and when the building suddenly collapses, he falls into a rage of such violence that he is finally driven mad. The actors performed this scene with great gusto, hardly missing a line in the salvoes of abuse exchanged between the various characters, and by the end the moral was clear enough: money is not everything, or the wages of materialism are madness. It was an apt reminder in the commercial free-for-all of present-day Doha, made all the more telling by the fact that most of the actors were the children of the very businessmen satirized in the play.

The students' disillusion with certain contemporary developments is often accompanied

by a definite nostalgia for the past. They seem to sense that though their parents' lives were much tougher, they were also more relaxed, even on the whole more agreeable. The country's official historian at the Emiri Palace finds that students often come to him to ask about pearl diving. 'They do not even know the vocabulary of the pearl trade, but they want to find out the details, what a particular boat was called and so on,' he says.

Some of the most popular plays produced by the theatre groups have dealt with the old way of life. *Umm el-Zein,* written by Abdel Rahman Mannai, a former Shell employee who is now head of the cultural centre, drew a parallel between the sea and oil, the old and new sources of wealth, and how both could be destructive. This was the play which had the record-breaking run of fourteen nights.

The same nostalgia can be found in the paintings of Jassem Zeini, the son of Muhammad the carpet merchant in the *souk.* Jassem has the imposing title of Deputy Director of Tourism and Antiquities, but his real interest is painting. His themes are taken from the past. One of his pictures shows a fisherman and a falconer, the two traditional Arab hunters on sea and land. Another is of a boy and girl, painted in almost Byzantine style, symbolizing an intimacy which no longer exists in modern life. Yet another shows a street scene with some people recovering a neighbour's lost sheep, an unimaginable event today in Doha's streamlined boulevards.

Jassem is now at work on a giant mural depicting Qatar's past and present which will hang on the walls of the new Ministry of Information. At thirty-nine, he is too young to have more than a vague memory of some of the subjects he paints. But obviously they exist vividly in his imagination, and reflect an anxiety about what is happening today which is shared by many younger Qataris. In ten or twenty years' time they will inherit the country being built around them now. What they will do with it depends largely on their capacity to adapt and consolidate in a rapidly changing society.

113

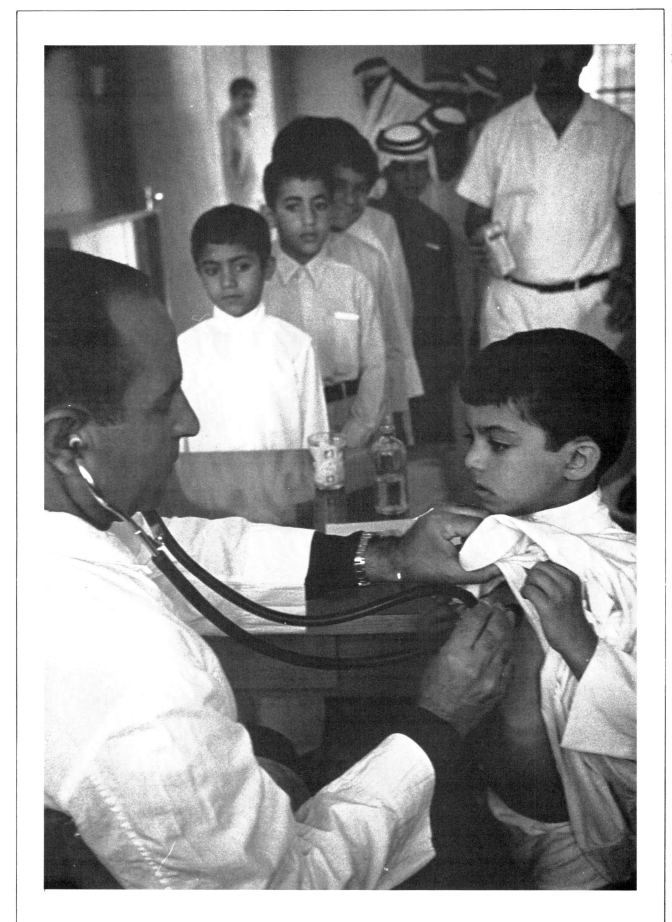

Photograph by Gérard Klijn

114

The Desert

'The men live by the sea, and for much of the year upon it; the towns and villages turn their backs, as it were, on the barren land' – *A Handbook of Arabia*, Vol. I, published by the British Admiralty (May 1916)

Inside Doha it is quite possible to forget the existence of the desert. The urban sprawl conceals the natural landscape and a visitor who never strayed outside the city might leave unaware of the wilderness that lies beyond the furthest house. It is only when you drive out of Doha that you see the place in perspective for the first time. Most cities ebb away into the surrounding countryside. Here the desert begins where the city ends. The last avenue of newly planted trees dies out, the modern buildings fall away, and there before you lies the flat stony plain stretching to the horizon in every direction for over 4,000 square miles. It is at this moment that you see Doha for what it is: a precarious enclave of human settlement on the edge of a harsh and barren land.

The stranger's first reaction to the arid scene is one of disbelief. It seems impossible that a view could be so empty, so completely lacking in any distinctive feature. The eye searches the horizon for a physical detail to relieve the monotony and finds nothing. And it is much the same across the length and breadth of the whole peninsula. There are seldom any of those variations in scenery which occasionally break up the uniformity of most other deserts, as do the mountain ranges in the Sahara or the vast rolling sand dunes of the Empty Quarter in Saudi Arabia. Where features do occur, it is in a minor key. The escarpment of low hills and wind-eroded ridges running down the west coast is no more than a brief interruption; the highest point is scarcely 300 feet above sea level and beyond

it a similar rock-strewn, though sandier plain continues south as far as the Saudi border, and west until it finally disappears into the sea. North of Doha the desert is relatively more fertile. Small date plantations occur quite frequently, and sometimes after the winter rains, patches of grass spring up on the plain in such profusion that through half-closed eyes you could almost create a mirage of green fields. But the effect is short-lived, and for nine tenths of the year the north is as bleak as any other part of Qatar.

Only the sand dunes on the east coast stand out in this landscape, although they are insignificant compared with the giant mounds of the Empty Quarter. If one travels south from Doha past the new industrial complex at Umm Said, one suddenly sees some oddly contoured shapes looming up on the plain. Standing there alone, these phenomena look completely out of place. Sometimes there is just a single dune rising for sixty or seventy feet in a solid mass from the floor of the desert. At first sight there seems to be no explanation for their existence unless someone had dumped huge loads of sand at random in the desert.

Each dune has a gently rising slope on one side and a steep face dropping abruptly from the summit on the other. In the early morning and late evening one side of the dune is cast into deep shadow by the sun shining horizontally across the desert. The resulting contrast between light and shadow, and the sinuous curves of their ridges, gives these dunes a sculptured beauty which can be found nowhere else in Qatar.

They do not always stay in the same place. Dunes are formed by the wind, which picks up grains of sand and bounces them along the hard surface of the desert. When the sand meets an obstacle such as a boulder, or comes to a soft patch of ground where the grains do not bounce

so high, it begins to accumulate. Slowly a
mound builds up, and as it increases in size, so
the sand trickles down the steep face away from
the wind, taking the mound on a few milli-
metres. In this way the dunes travel surrepti-
tiously across the desert, sometimes moving as
far as twenty or thirty metres a year. They are
often visited by the people of Doha, who drive
out with their families on a holiday and spend
the afternoon tobogganing down the steep
banks of smooth yellow sand.

Further south, around the inland sea at Khor
al Odeid, there are larger dunes shaped like
crescents. Linked together for mile after mile,
they stretch right down to the shoreline in loops
and curves like heavy snowdrifts. Between them
lie the white patches of *sabka*, or salt flats, whose
steady increase over the years indicates that
Qatar is slowly drying up.

This, then, is the uncompromising hinterland
of the city which has sprung up so rapidly on the
east coast. It is no wonder that in the past the
people turned their backs on the interior and
trusted in the sea to support them. Yet the
Qatari desert, like all deserts, has a subtlety and a
beauty which is not apparent at first sight.
Details which are obvious to the experienced eye
are hidden from the newcomer, and it is only
when he has lived in the desert for a time that he
begins to notice how it is a place of startling
contrasts: how a slight depression can conceal
a whole group of people in an apparently open
landscape; how even the smallest hill casts a
long shadow over the plain in the evening sun;
and how at dawn the mist hangs in the hollows
and for a while reduces the vast horizons of
daytime to more intimate dimensions. These
are things known to every Qatari, for despite
the lure of the city the desert is still very much
part of his life.

The Bedouin

At first sight there are few traces of human activity in the desert. Here and there the imprint of modern development has left its mark: a dual carriageway streaking across the plain or a line of pylons disappearing over the horizon. But these, like the abandoned rusty cars beside the road, are no more than superficial blemishes on an untouched landscape, and apart from a few dusty villages, one can travel for miles without seeing a sign of another human being. But the desert is full of people – more, probably, than there have ever been in the past. This is partly because it is more accessible: a two-day camel journey has become a one-hour car drive; and partly because the Bedouin instinct of a people who now live mostly in the city is still very strong.

The Bedouin have been as much part of Qatar's history as the fishermen and pearl divers who lived in the villages. Indeed, the people who first settled on the coast were themselves Bedouin in origin. Others remained nomadic and continued to visit the market towns of Doha and Wakrah, where they sold their camels and goats in return for food and cloth. Each tribe had its own rights and insignia, instantly recognizable to the others. Their livestock, and sometimes even their falcons, were branded with a tribal mark known as a *wasm*. The sign of the Manasir, for instance, was a line with a dot on either side; the Bani Hajir identified their property by two small circles, one on top of the other. Sometimes these tribal marks were carved on wells as a clear warning for others to keep away. Several such places can still be seen today, and there is at least one well on the Saudi border named after the Bani Hajir.

It was an austere but self-reliant way of life. The animals were sufficient for nearly all the tribesmen's needs. They provided milk and meat for the occasional feast. Goat's hair was woven into tents, camel hair into ropes, bags and cloaks. Sheep's wool was turned into blankets and rugs. Beyond these things, all that was required was a little water. If there was enough water, then the Bedouin were practically immune to the economic vagaries of the outside world such as the depression in the West which helped to destroy the pearl trade. They could endure any amount of hardship; what they could not survive was affluence.

There are three different kinds of Bedouin in Qatar today: first, the genuine nomads; secondly, the part-time Bedouin who have been settled by the government but who every now and then abandon their homes and their jobs and for a while resume the nomadic life; and finally, the 'weekend' Bedouin, who are completely settled and make brief excursions to the desert much as an Englishman visits his country cottage.

Not many of the truly nomadic Bedouin are left in Qatar, and those who do remain have changed their style of life completely. They still move freely between Saudi Arabia and Qatar, usually migrating up the western coast of the peninsula in the cool season. National borders mean nothing to them, and few even own a passport. But now they arrive more like Western campers than nomads, cruising across the desert in a Land-Rover or pick-up. In their baggage they carry with them the traditional long-nosed coffee pots and rugs, but they will also have a radio, a television set or the standard tartan suitcase.

The camel, once the lifeline of the Bedouin's existence, is no longer essential to the tribesmen. There are still plenty of camels in Qatar outside the towns: a 1974 animal census counted no less than 8,148, which is considerably more than Lorimer discovered seventy years ago. Most of them can be found in the south, and on the road to Saudi Arabia occasional 'Camels Crossing'

Qatari girls reading the Koran.

signs warn drivers of their erratic appearance on the highway. Camels are not usually restricted to their village or Bedouin camp. They wander freely in the open, often with their front feet tied together to prevent them straying too far. Each animal is still marked with the tribal brand of its owner so that everyone knows to whom it belongs. Nevertheless, the camel has now sadly lost its purpose. The ship of the desert has become a pet, seldom ridden and kept only for its milk and out of a sentimental attachment to the past in the same way that the old pearl diver still goes back to the pearl banks.

Yet, despite everything – the redundant camels, the motorized transport, the supermarket gadgets – these Bedouin remain genuinely nomadic. They have no jobs, no permanent homes, and their children do not go to school. It is a way of life which cannot last much longer. Sooner or later the more settled society which is gradually encroaching on their independence will absorb them. Many of them have already succumbed to the temptations of city life. And those who have so far resisted find it difficult to ignore the benefits of the government's policy of settling the people. Apart from the housing estates in Doha, new towns are being built in other parts of the peninsula in an attempt to spread the population more evenly around the country. The main one is Madinat al Shamal, or the North City, near the old pearling village of Ruwais. Further south, Al Ka'aaban, Ghuwairiyah and Al Shahaniyeh are already taking shape.

These new towns, with their modern houses, electricity and water have attracted people from the surrounding countryside where such facilities are not available. Along the north-west coast whole communities have packed up and left their villages. Abandoned by their owners, the houses quickly succumb to the wind and sand, and soon the whole village is reclaimed by the desert. At Al Jumail, once a small fishing centre, one man remains. All the rest of the inhabitants recently moved to the new township of Abu Dluf. The man who stayed behind is employed as a guard for an industrial installation close by. Once a week he goes to Ruwais to buy provisions. At night he sleeps in one of the decaying houses, and every day in the afternoon he walks back from his work to pray in the village mosque. The wind whistles through the open windows and a door bangs endlessly on its hinges, but he seems oblivious to the mournful solitude of the place.

Elsewhere the government's intervention has in some cases saved a dying community. Almariya, a few miles off the road to Abu Dhabi, is such a place. Thirty years ago it was a Bedouin encampment. Two or three hundred people lived in tents and looked after their sheep and camels. When the rains failed they drove their flocks as far as Abu Dhabi and Kuwait in search of grazing. Then came oil and people started drifting away to Doha. Soon there were only a few families left, and it seemed certain that Almariya would disappear. But at this point the government stepped in. Electricity was brought to the village, a motorized pump was installed to raise water from the well and financial assistance was given to anyone who wished to build a house. Today over a hundred people live in Almariya. It is not an especially prosperous or attractive spot. There are no trees, not even a small date grove. The whitewashed houses are scattered over a wide stony area as barren as anywhere in the whole Qatari desert. But it has survived, and the people are determined to stay.

Muhammad Ali was born there about fifty years ago and his life is a microcosm of everything that has happened to Qatar in that time. As a boy he used to look after his father's animals. The family owned 50 camels and 120 sheep, and sometimes Muhammad used to accompany his father on long expeditions into the Saudi interior. When the oil companies returned after the war, he found a job as a bulldozer driver in Dukhan. But he always came back to Almariya, and as soon as the government offered to help, he built a house there. Today he is a prosperous man. In the week days he works as a driver in Doha, where he owns another house. At weekends he drives back to Almariya to join his family. His rooms are wallpapered and the floors are covered with carpets and bright-coloured brass-studded elbow rests. He still owns twenty camels and a

few sheep, and when visitors arrive unexpectedly, he slaughters and skins a lamb with his own hands to provide a feast for them. He has three brothers, one in the civil service, one in the army and one employed by an oil company. He also has a son who goes to school in Karana twenty miles away. 'When he grows up he will have a thousand more opportunities than I ever had,' says Muhammad, 'but he will always come back here when he needs to feel free.'

It is the loss of that sense of freedom which turns people in the new towns into part-time nomads. The government tries hard to provide what they need. Jobs are well-paid, and the housing estates are designed to accommodate their possessions. Many of the houses include a

compound for the livestock which the families bring with them when they move in. On some estates a 'neighbourhood shepherd' is employed by the community to look after the animals in the daytime. When the shepherd returns in the evening, he throws a stone into the middle of the communal flock, and the animals separate into groups and trot off to the houses of their respective owners.

But it takes time to adapt to a settled way of life, and every so often a man will suddenly leave his job and his home to wander off into the desert. No private business or government department is free from this experience, and most of them treat it as an occupational hazard. One day the driver is there: the next he has mysteriously vanished, only to reappear again in six months' time to resume his duties as though nothing had happened. This occurs quite frequently among the coastguards and police whose ranks are filled with former Bedouin. And even when the urge to take off is dormant, a chance invitation to join a month's hunting expedition can prove irresistible.

There is hardly a Qatari, in fact, who does not still regard the desert as his proper home. On a Friday morning, the week's work completed, he will pack his family into the car with an ample supply of food and drive off to some spot he has probably been visiting for years. In the winter the desert can seem almost crowded. All along the highway from Doha to Dukhan there are cars parked a few hundred yards off the road, apparently at random, their bonnets gleaming in the bright sun. These are the 'weekend' Bedouin enjoying their leisure. Some of them will be quite simple people, others may have sophisticated jobs and travel abroad, but all share the same instincts which lead them back to the open spaces.

One afternoon on the way back from Dukhan we joined a group setting up camp about half a mile from the road. The spot they had chosen was a shallow depression with a few scrub bushes and a covering of fresh grass which had sprung up after the recent rain. They had arrived from Doha about an hour before, and already the long black-and-white-striped tents were in place. A pick-up appeared and disgorged its load of goats and sheep. The women

Repairing nets

Omani fisherman

Dhows, Doha

Museum piece, Doha

Fishing fleet

Dhows

Museum piece, Doha

Museum keeper

Museum piece, Doha

Bedouin feast

retired to the impenetrable privacy of their quarters while the men and a few curious children gathered in a circle on the brightly coloured carpets of their tent to drink tea and coffee. Occasionally others appeared from near-by tents and quietly joined the circle.

These people all had Bedouin origins, and many had spent their childhood as nomads. They belonged to the Al Morra, one of the tribes which has been wandering in and out of Qatar for centuries and which was once described by an English writer as 'the wildest, most dangerous of nomad tribes in Eastern Arabia'. Tribal affiliations are disappearing in modern Qatar, but most people, particularly those of Bedouin stock, can still tell you the name of their tribe and the exact branch or subdivision to which their family belongs. Nowadays the fierce reputation of the Al Morra is no more than a memory. The rampaging nomadic life has been exchanged for a quiet suburb in Doha, and the nearest they get to the wild adventures of the past is the occasional excursion to the desert at weekends, and for longer periods in the spring. Their children are educated in the city

and some of the young men will take up a career in oil or industry. When their families are camping, the children commute between the city and the desert. It takes less than forty minutes by car – a short journey between the past and the present.

The family, with the unstinting hospitality shown by nearly all Bedouin, invited us to come back for lunch, so next day we returned to find a lamb had been slaughtered in our honour. One of the most remarkable things about the Bedouin is that no matter how long it is since they abandoned the nomadic life, they still seem to observe the customs of their ancestors down to the last meticulous detail. The tents are still woven by women from goat's hair, coffee and tea are still brewed on the traditional pots in the sand, and visitors are entertained in the same extravagant style.

These habits are as familiar to the young as the old, and, for most of them, the experience of desert life is just as real. Nearly every Qatari boy, for instance, goes out hunting at some time or other. They still use falcons, though not as much as rifles, and as game becomes scarcer in

White oryx

Qatar, expeditions travel further and further afield. One sixteen-year-old boy in the camp had just returned from a two-month hunting trip to Syria. The party had consisted of 300 men and 85 cars, and they had killed deer, bustards and even a few wolves. The boy went to school in Doha, and said he wanted to be an ambassador when he grew up, but in some ways he was more at home in the desert.

One animal which can no longer be hunted is the Arabian oryx. This beautiful creature has a fawn-coloured coat at birth, which turns white by the time it is a year old. It is smaller than the African oryx and has shorter horns. When seen in profile it appears to have only one horn, an illusion which supposedly gave rise to the legend of the unicorn. Fifty years ago the oryx was to be found all over the desert of the Arabian peninsula. But after the Second World War it was hunted to the point of extinction by expeditions travelling in Land-Rovers and armed with automatic weapons. Today it is almost certain that the sole survivors are in captivity. Only a very few herds have been successfully raised away from their natural state, and one of them is in Qatar. It owes its existence entirely to the enterprise of the late Sheikh Jasim bin Hamad, the present Ruler's brother. In 1964 Jasim captured three oryx on the edge of the Empty Quarter in Saudi Arabia and brought them back to Qatar. Over the years he made further expeditions and added to their numbers. Jasim died a few years ago, but the oryx have been maintained on an estate in the north of the peninsula. The herd is strictly protected. At the last count it consisted of thirty-four oryx, almost the only ones left in the whole of Arabia.

Lunch that day with the Bedouin was an elaborate affair which lasted well over three hours. When the meal was finished the men rose to their feet and wandered off into the desert to say their prayers, leaving the camp empty and silent. The only sounds were the braying of the goats and the tents flapping in the afternoon breeze. For a moment one had some faint idea what these people meant when they talked about the freedom of the desert. Only half a mile away the traffic streamed down the road to Dukhan. But that was another world: here, in the open, one might have been back in the days before oil was discovered.

The Fishing Villages

The same sense of the past can be found in the old fishing villages around the coast. There are not many of them left. In some places the shoreline stretches for mile after mile without a trace of life, and nothing interrupts the symmetry of sea and sand. The water washes endlessly against the beaches and the beaches merge imperceptibly into the desert with no more than a fringe of debris to distinguish them. Occasionally the ruins of some long-abandoned pearling village appear on the edge of a bay, the crumbling grey houses barely discernible against the stony background. Many villages died with the pearl trade, but others survived by fishing, a trade older than pearling itself. There is now a faded air about these places, almost as though they were superfluous in a country which lives on oil.

The oldest and strangest of them is Wakrah, a town only ten minutes' drive south of Doha. In Arabic the name means 'Falcon's Perch', and fifty years ago Wakrah was second only to Doha, a thriving market and fishing town with 8,000 people. An English visitor reported that in 1915 it possessed 75 shops, 200 boats, 150 camels and 40 horses. Half a mile inland the local sheikhs had built a huge rectangular fort.

The fort is still there, standing shuttered and unused a few yards from the dual carriageway which runs up to Doha. Wakrah itself is a curious blend between the aggressive present and the decaying past. Along the seafront the old town lies in total ruins, as though it had been devastated by an earthquake or a bombing attack. But these ruins are merely the ravages of neglect. Once there were many fine merchant houses, but now all that is left of them is the occasional beautifully carved doorway or rounded arch imprisoned among piles of fallen masonry. A few people still live in this urban graveyard, and, rounding a corner, one sometimes comes across a shiny Japanese car parked incongruously in the

crumbling alleyways. Everyone else has moved to the modern housing estates rising around the perimeter of the old town. For the new Wakrah has become a dormitory town for commuters working in Doha. Down on the seafront a jetty is being built, and all day long a stream of heavy lorries treks through the rubble of the old town with materials for the new. You do not see any camels here, and the pearling fleet has long since been turned to firewood. Only a few fishing boats remain moored on the off-shore sand-bank.

Ironically, Wakrah and the neighbouring village of Wuqair ten miles inland are the most conservative places in the whole country. The local sheikhs have always resisted change. They fear that schools, television and all the other aspects of the modern state will undermine their old way of life. Even now there are more mosques in Wuqair than television sets. The inhabitants are very proud of their independence, but soon they too, like the Bedouin, will be enveloped by the modern age.

Further up the coast, the village of Al Khor has retained its character more obviously than either Wakrah or Doha. A few cranes and concrete mixers have started work, and parts of the desert have already been staked out with breezeblocks. But it is still a small fishing community, much as Doha used to be twenty-five years ago. The village stands in the middle of a wide sheltered bay where scores of dhows ride at their moorings. Others are drawn up on the beach, undergoing repairs.

Here, as in other villages in Qatar, the fishing industry has changed little over the years. The state now owns a small fleet of modern trawlers which catches prawns for export to the United States and Japan. But the traditional methods continue. The fishermen of Al Khor have prospered and they own more dhows today than

139

they did seventy years ago. A few are still built locally, while the rest come from Dubai and Bahrain. Sails have given way to engines and the fishing nets are no longer made by hand. But otherwise the daily chores are much the same as ever. The fisherman sitting on the beach at Al Khor mends his nets exactly as his ancestors did before him. Oil has done little to change his way of life.

Nowhere is this more obvious than in the remote village of Da'sa on the western coast of Qatar. Here, on an empty stretch of beach a few miles from the Dukhan oil field, there comes every winter a group of Omani fishermen. These are the Bedouin of the sea. Each year they leave their homes for several months and sail up the Gulf, stopping at various points along the coast to cast their nets. They make this journey because there are too many fishermen in Oman and they can get a better price for their catch in places like Abu Dhabi and Qatar. For a few weeks the men live on the beach in primitive barrasti huts and sell their fish to the local people. Then, one day, as summer approaches, they are gone, only to return next year to the same place at the same time. It is a very ancient routine and it will probably still be going on long after the last oil tanker has sailed from the Gulf.

A short distance away from the huts of the Omani fishermen, one of the oil wells of the Dukhan field has been sunk in the desert. From the beach it is hardly visible. A protective barrier surrounds a compact installation of pipes and bolts covering no more than a few square yards. The well is not guarded, and even when the oil is flowing it makes very little noise. This unobtrusive structure looks quite inadequate for its task, but is in fact perfectly efficient. Once the wells have been drilled, the roads built and the pipelines completed, oil production is a tidy and economic business. That stage was passed some time ago in Qatar, and what remains is remarkably inconspicuous – not much more than a few oil wells and their connecting pipelines snaking across the desert. Fewer than 2,000 men are employed in the whole industry, including the off-shore oil fields.

That so few people and so little visible machinery is needed to underwrite the economy of a whole country seems almost inconceivable. But they do. Nine tenths of Qatar's national income is derived from oil, and nowadays that represents a very considerable amount of money. In 1939, just before the outbreak of war, Sheikh Abdulla, who was no doubt concerned about the future, asked for his annual payment to be made in cash. The total sum came to 163,250 rupees, or about £20,000. By 1951, when the oil had started to flow, the revenue had increased to nearly £2 million. These sums seem trivial compared with today's figures, which run into thousands of millions of pounds a year.

The oil comes from two main sources: one on land, the other off-shore. The Dukhan field on the west coast has been in operation since 1949. The sea off Dukhan is too shallow for tankers to approach the shore, so the oil is pumped for sixty miles across the desert to the terminal at Umm Said. The off-shore fields lie about fifty miles from the east coast of the peninsula. This is where much of the pearling used to be done and the oil companies did not forget it: the three biggest fields – Idd al Shargi, Maydan Mahzam and Bul Hanine – were all called after pearl banks, and although the names do not correspond exactly, they provide a rare instance of continuity in modern Qatar. Each field is linked to the island of Halul, where the oil is stored in giant containers awaiting export. The first one only started operating in the middle 1960s, but already off-shore production accounts for as much if not more than Dukhan. The oil is of high quality and now completely owned by the state. There is also another field called Bunduq which is jointly shared with Abu Dhabi.

Such are the reservoirs of Qatar's wealth, and they do not include the enormous deposits of gas which may in the end turn out to be even more valuable than the oil. Nobody is quite sure how long the bonanza will last. A popular prediction is about thirty years, but that is based on the 1973 production rate, which has since dropped sharply. And if more oil was to be found in other parts of the country, the reserves would obviously last much longer.

The pioneers who set up the oil camp in Dukhan before the war could scarcely have envisaged the sheer volume of natural resources waiting to be tapped. There was nothing there when they first arrived: no water wells, no villages, hardly even a passing Bedouin. Everything had to be brought in. The heavy machinery was shipped to Doha and then taken overland by a rough desert track. The sixty-mile journey took three hours by car; today it takes just under an hour. Food and water came by dhow from Bahrain to a jetty which was built a few miles north of Dukhan at Bir Zekrit. The mail for Doha also came by dhow and was then taken on by camel. Letters posted in Bahrain usually arrived in Doha five days later.

The opening of the Dukhan oil field provided some much-needed work for the local people, many of whom were by then half-starving and unemployed. Workers were recruited through the Ruler's office and paid one and a half rupees a day. They lived in the oil camp and returned to their homes at weekends. Every Thursday afternoon families gathered in the centre of Doha to meet the convoys of trucks and trailers bringing the workers back from Dukhan. Some of the men then travelled on to their homes in Fuwairet, Abu Dluf and other villages in the north. On Friday evenings they reassembled at the pick-up point in Doha and returned to the oil camp.

The local work-force was supplemented by immigrants from India, Pakistan and various Arab countries. These men were all skilled workers, and their employers went to some trouble to prepare them for the rough conditions they would find at Dukhan. A contract note issued on 19 November 1952 to an applicant from Bombay made the following points:

Water
Water is normally available in adequate quantity but has on occasions to be rationed. The Qatar peninsula has no natural recreational facility other than hiking and sea bathing. Personnel from larger towns will miss the social activities normal to city life.

Messing Arrangements
Owing to the complete absence of bazaar or shopping centre, due to desert conditions, food is provided ready cooked at reasonable rates. It is not possible for employees to purchase rations and prepare their own food.

Legal and Social Position
The following are forbidden by the Government of Qatar:—
i)   Possession of alcohol
ii) Playing of musical instruments
iii) Gambling

The spectacle of a party of Pakistani workers hiking across the burning desert on their days off is a little difficult to imagine, but there were at least some compensations for the immigrants in their exile. Accommodation was free, there was a tobacconist in the camp and a cinema had just been opened.

Twenty-five years later, Dukhan is a very different place. Compared with the restless bustle of Doha it seems calm and orderly, like one of those shanty-towns in a gold rush which, after the first wave of hectic exploitation, settle down and become respectable. The disused airfield survives as a reminder of the pioneer days, but otherwise Dukhan looks more like a suburban industrial estate than an oil camp. Everything is neat and tidy. There is an outdoor cinema and rows of compact little houses built in straight lines. When the employees finish work for the day, they can jump in their cars and drive to the nine-hole golf course carved out of the desert a few hundred yards away. The fairways, made out of sand treated with crude oil, are black, and the greens brown. A straight-faced notice beside the first tee gives the following warning: 'IN ORDER TO MAINTAIN THE BROWNS IN GOOD CONDITION HEELED AND/OR ROUGH SOLED SHOES ARE NOT ALLOWED ON THE COURSE'. When it rains the course is unplayable because the oil separates from the sand and the browns become a sticky mess.

Most of the staff now live in Doha, commuting to and from the oil field in their own cars or by taxi at the company's expense. They are

Aerial view of port at Doha

Aerial view of Doha

Aerial view of National Museum, Doha

Cup presentation, Doha

IN ORDER TO MAINTAIN THE BROWNS IN GOOD CONDITION HEELED AND/ OR ROUGH SOLED SHOES ARE NOT ALLOWED ON THE COURSE

Industrial complex, Umm Said

The links, Dukhan

all well paid: the basic rate for an ordinary worker is nearly 40 riyals (about £6) a day – more than twenty-five times what it used to be. Many of the younger Qataris have made their career in oil. Muhammad Bakhit al Kawari, a thirty-nine-year-old clerk, has been working in Dukhan since 1955. His family were fishermen and pearl divers in the village of Fuwairet, which is now almost deserted. Muhammad was one of the early recruits to the oil camp, where he started work at 5 rupees a day. Now he lives in Doha, occasionally returning to the village where he was born with a picnic which he eats among the empty houses. The experience leaves him unmoved: life in Fuwairet was too hard to arouse any nostalgia for him.

Perhaps the strangest place around Dukhan is the village of Bir Zekrit, close to the jetty where the dhows used to arrive with provisions for the oil camp. You reach it by driving north from the main office buildings, leaving the disused airfield on the right. A little further on the road passes over several pipelines which zig-zag away across the desert to the east. When they are first installed, these pipes are black and shiny, but the wind and sand soon turn them into a rusty brown. They are bent deliberately to stop them cracking in the summer heat. Beyond the pipeline the road runs dead straight for about a mile and then ends abruptly in a small settlement of ramshackle houses. This is Bir Zekrit. Here the notorious pirate Rahmah bin Jabir once built a fort, but not even the ruins remain today.

The village grew up with the oil field, and nearly all the inhabitants used to work at Dukhan. Now they are drifting away to Doha, and of the eleven families still there, only three are employed by the oil company. The others make a living by driving the local children to and from the schools in the district, a task for which they are paid by the ever-bountiful government. As the people leave, Bir Zekrit declines, but in a far more depressing fashion than those abandoned villages on the north coast. For this place was touched by affluence, however lightly, and signs of it remain. An electric generator still provides power, and several houses have television aerials rising from their corrugated-iron roofs. A dozen cars are scattered around among the sheep and goats which wander through the village. The old stone well has fallen in and water arrives every day by tanker. Beyond the well an expertly built drystone wall shows that someone once tried to make something of the place. But nowadays it is a desolate spot, especially in the winter when the north wind blows in fiercely from the sea. Like the disused airfield down the road, Bir Zekrit has outlived its purpose. It was no more than a landmark on Qatar's road to prosperity; and now that the oil for which it was built has been secured, it will soon surely disappear.

Agriculture and Industry

Forty miles north of Doha, just off the main road to Madinat al Shamal, there is a place where you can stand in a long avenue of trees and not even know you are in the desert. It is a peculiar sensation to arrive at this fertile spot from the empty and barren land all around. For a time, everything seems out of place, and then slowly one grows used to the rich variety of sounds and smells which do not exist in the desert: the wind swishing through the tree-tops, birds calling and the buzzing of insects attracted by the vegetation. The deeply cracked soil

Fruits of the desert

Irrigation

reflects the intensity of the sun, but only when you look over the thick hedges which surround this oasis do you realize how close the desert is.

Rodait al Khail is an experimental farm and one example of how the oil revenues are being spent. The government's aim is to make the country self-supporting in food and, improbable though it may seem, Qatar already does export vegetables: every year, for instance, 150 tons of locally grown tomatoes are sold abroad. The 130-acre farm is worked by Qatari managers and immigrant labourers. Here tests are carried out on a variety of crops to find those most suitable for the climate. Grapes, figs, melons, marrows and at least four different types of radish flourish with such success that the local date tree may soon find itself in the Garden of Eden. The farm is self-sufficient in water and fertilizers are used to reduce the salinity of the soil.

Twenty years ago there was hardly an acre of cultivated land in Qatar, but today Rodait al Khail is only one of nearly 500 farms in the country. Many of these are privately owned and receive assistance from the state. Tractor ploughing, seeds and pesticides are all provided free. A whole range of livestock is being imported to join the indigenous camel. At Umm Qarn, twenty miles north of Doha, a poultry farm will soon be producing 10 million eggs and a million broilers a year. Cattle and sheep farms have already been planned.

All these projects, and indeed every enterprise in the country, depends on water, a commodity which is as valuable to Arabia as oil is to Europe. Qatar is a very arid place. It has no surface water and until recently relied on the wells scattered across the desert for its supplies. This water is not salty, like Bahrain's, but it is scarce, and in the last few years the underground reservoirs have been falling quickly. Even so, they have

only provided a third of the country's needs. The solution to this problem was to tap the resources of the sea, an expensive process but one which Qatar can well afford. The first desalination plant was built in 1957 at Ras Abu Abboud. A second one at Ras Abu Fontas is now almost finished, and when it goes into operation the two plants will be producing 40 million gallons of desalinated water a day.

The trouble is that demand is forever threatening to overtake supply, not least because of the ambitious programme of industrial diversification which the country has embarked upon. This programme is designed to ensure a future for Qatar when the oil runs out. Already it is well under way. At Umm Bab on the west coast, a new cement works is being built to supplement the existing plant. By 1980 more than 2,000 tons will be produced daily, enough, one imagines, to satisfy even the voracious demands of Doha's construction industry.

But the centrepiece of the blueprint is Umm Said on the east coast where the oil terminal is sited. Here a huge industrial complex is taking shape and there are plans for a town housing 15,000 people near by. Among the projects either completed or in the pipeline, there is an oil refinery, a petrochemical plant, some flour mills, an iron and steel mill, and a fertilizer company which exports to countries as far apart as Turkey and Vietnam. Altogether it represents an investment of around £750 million over the next ten years.

It is indeed an ambitious plan. Its viability in the long term will depend on a great number of factors, notably the supply of manpower and the existence of necessary markets for all the new industrial products. When one looks back at the history of the area one has to wonder, except that today's astonishing prosperity is built on firmer foundations. The industrial

Industrial complex, Umm Said

projects and agricultural experiments seem to be taking root in a land in which they are completely alien. The bureaucrats and businessmen of Doha are already transforming the country, and soon the younger generation of Qataris will emerge from the schools and universities to take up what they have begun.

But to the traveller who flies over the country the signs of human activity seem almost inconspicuous. The oil-storage tanks at Umm Said look no larger than miniature flying saucers, and in the north the oases of cultivation seem to occupy no more space than a few missing pieces in a jigsaw puzzle. Around them stretches the unchanging austerity of the desert. All one can say is that the new world taking shape below is clearly in defiance of the elements.

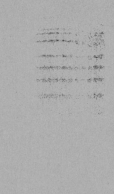